WITHDRAWN

Black
Voices
from
Prison

BLACK VOICES FROM PRISON

BY ETHERIDGE KNIGHT

and other inmates of
Indiana State Prison

With an Introduction by
Roberto Giammanco

A MERIT BOOK

PATHFINDER PRESS, INC.
NEW YORK 1970

Manufactured in the United States of America
Library of Congress Catalog Card Number 79-96955

First Edition, April 1970
Second Printing, September 1970
Third Printing, December 1971

Original title: *Voci Negre Dal Carcere,* published in 1968 by
Gius. Laterza & Figli, Bari, Italy.

Acknowledgments:

*For permission to reprint copyrighted material the following
acknowledgments are gratefully made to:*
Broadside Press, for the poems "Cell Song," "To Make a
Poem in Prison," "Hard Rock Returns to Prison from the Hos-
pital for the Criminal Insane," "The Warden Said to Me the
Other Day," "The Idea of Ancestry," "For Freckle-Faced Ger-
ald," and "He Sees Through Stone," which appeared in *Poems
From Prison* by Etheridge Knight, copyright © 1968.
Greater Works, publishers, for the poem "A WASP Woman
Visits a Black Junkie in Prison," copyright © *Greater Works*
issue of March 1966.
McGraw-Hill Book Co., for selections from *Soul on Ice* by
Eldridge Cleaver, copyright © 1968 by Eldridge Cleaver. Used
with permission of McGraw-Hill Book Co.
Pantheon Books, a division of Random House, Inc., for
selections from *The Schoolchildren* by Mary F. Greene and
Orletta Ryan, copyright © 1964.

PATHFINDER PRESS
410 West Street
New York, N.Y. 10014

Preface

by Etheridge Knight

Malcolm X once remarked to an audience in Detroit: "Don't be shocked when I say that I was in prison. You're still in prison. That's what America means: prison." A natural fact. From the time the first of our fathers were bound and shackled and herded into the dark hold of a "Christian" slaveship—right on up to the present day, the whole experience of the black man in America can be summed up in one word: prison.

Prison.
    Locked doors.
        Barred windows.
        Moon nights.
        Fire eyes flare.
Prison.
    Locked doors.
        Dark holes.
        Chains clang.
        Hounds howl.
Sheets of flame shimmer in the back of the brain.

Everywhere it is said that "crime" is rising; and everywhere there are the prison walls, growing higher and

higher. Walls—we live in a world of walls: from the
wall of racism that shut Martin Luther King out of
Gage Park, Illinois, to the walls of fire in Vietnam and
Newark, to the gray stone walls of San Quentin. And
it is all too clear that there is a direct relationship between men behind prison walls and men behind the
myriad walls that permeate this society. According to
the *Report by the President's Commission on Law
Enforcement and Administration of Justice*, "Crime is
a social problem that is interwoven with almost every
aspect of American life; controlling it involves changing
the way schools are run and classes are taught, the way
cities are built, the way businesses are managed and
workers are hired. Crime is a kind of human behavior;
controlling means changing the minds and hearts of
men."

To be more specific—this excessive amount of so-
called crime/criminality/alienation can be understood
as being the by-product of a society/culture whose tech-
nology has far outstripped its humanism, a society/
culture in which—by some feat of white magic and
white logic, the glory of Man was transferred to machines and to their products. This mechanized fucking
of humanity by perverted Europeans gave birth to
the French penal colonies, the British convict ships,
etc.; and these grotesque babies multiplied and spread
all over the world. Everywhere the master went, his
jails were sure to go.

In another, more pertinent sense, crime/criminality/
alienation is a matter of definition. And when a people
set out, with a gun in one hand and a Bible in the
other, to exploit and enslave and imprison all the other
peoples of the world (and succeed), and then the exploited and enslaved are called the criminals—it is time
to redefine terms. It is time to put the proper shoe
on the proper foot.

This book is a small attempt in that direction. It is
a collection of testaments, essays, short stories, poems,

and articles, most of which are by and about black
men who are imprisoned in this just one of the many
prisons that rise like sores over the skin of white/racist
America. Some of the "voices" included here were transcribed from tape recordings that were made by the
men alone in their cells. When it was suggested to them
that they might suffer some kind of reprisal for telling
it like it is, they—to a man—replied: "Fuckit—straight
ahead." And there is no doubt that some of them will
suffer some kind of reprisal from the "authorities."

No great effort has been made to present an "objective" view of prison/america but rather a *truthful*
view. And the "Testament" of Li'l David Flournoy is
the truth. He tells of his childhood in a Southern river
town, of his attempts to understand and cope with
this racist system's program of dehumanization. And
in his attempts to evade the nutcutting, David Flournoy
exploded. He said, *No*, and his *No* was a mad/uncool
adventure that led him to prison at twenty-four years
of age to serve—all at one time—a life sentence, 10-25,
2-21, 1-10, and 1-5 years.

> *Vengeance*
> *is mine,*
> *Saith the Law.*

Louis Bean is a white boy—a "po' white" boy. And
his "Testament" is also the truth. He tells of running
away from home, of spending time in juvenile institutions, and of finally picking up the gun—the unequivocal
No. On the prison scene, Louis Bean is known as
somewhat of a nigger-lover because he realizes that the
poor whites are exploited and enslaved along with the
blacks, and that ego-satisfying prejudices do not fill
empty bellies or balance the scales of the oppressor's
justice.

The voice of Charles Baker is the voice of a black

warrior: "What do *I* think of Malcolm? I love Malcolm."
In prison, he grew— became aware. He refuses to submit
to the devils/designs. When Charles Baker dies (and
death rides his back like a junkie's monkey), he will
die a warrior's death — standing on his feet, as Malcolm
stood — moving against the murderers who plot his
death and the death of his brothers.

> *sing no sad/*
> > *death songs for me*
> *and light no candles in my name*
> *sing war/chants*
> > *to my sons for me*
> *that they may die the same.*

To be in prison under any circumstance is a bitch,
but to be in prison and innocent of the charge is a
most muthafucka. "The Innocents" is an account of
two men, both presently imprisoned here, who have
spent long years behind bars for no other reasons
than circumstances and being black and poor. One
of the innocents, J. W. Prewitt, has from the outset
resisted the oppressor's Law and Justice, and so, like
Charles Baker, Prewitt is a candidate for the Law's
"final solution." By contrast, Donald Peck, the other
innocent, has accepted the "sanctity and dignity" of
the racist Law — and has been programmed into near
nonexistence.

> *wide eyes stare fat zeros*
> *and plea only for pity*

"The Innocents," as a classic example of the naked
brutality of a racist society and its Law, proves the
truth of the statement by Stokely Carmichael and Dr.
Charles V. Hamilton in their book *Black Power:* "Law
is the agent of those in political power; it is the product

of those powerful enough to define right and wrong and to have that definition legitimized by 'law.' This is not to say that 'might makes right,' but it is to say that Might makes Law."

Power equals Law equals Right as defined by whoever has got the guns and tear gas. Long before Mao Tse-tung came on the scene, the Man's game was tight: Commodore Perry sailed his gunboats into the Sea of Japan; Teddy Roosevelt swung his Big Stick throughout the Caribbean; Mayor Daley occupied Chicago; four days ago, one tier above me, young black men were tear-gassed and beaten while already locked in solitary confinement.

Prison is the ultimate in oppression. And as with black people in the larger prison outside, the keepers try to hold the black inmates' minds in chains along with their bodies by making full use of a white educational system, a white communications system, a dead white Art, and the white Law. But the soul-killing effect of a racist culture on black inmates has been greatly offset by the phenomenal rise of black consciousness, even though the keepers, via the "kangaroo court" and the "goon squad," move to obstruct and destroy this blossoming consciousness. In "The Day the Young Blacks Came" I have presented a collection of letters written/smuggled to me by young black men, most of whom are yet confined on "The Rock." In discussing these letters and black consciousness with a friend in the outside world, I wrote:

"You will notice, I'm sure, that even though these letters *are* repetitions of often voiced indignities and injustices, they are not grievances, in the usual sense. They are indictments.

"These cats (most of them are under twenty-five) make no apologies for being who they are; and, though they accept — up to a certain point — their own personal responsibilities for being here, they no longer accept whitey's definition of their selves. They use a new frame of reference. And in spite of the tyrannical character of prison, without bowing or whining and without much hope, they somehow manage to keep body and spirit intact. Prison usually breaks men, but not these cats; they are a new breed of convict. Unlike the old convicts who sink lead-like into a sea of inertia, these young men *think* and *feel*—regardless of the accompanying pain. They are restless; they emit a great energy wherever they gather, on the Yard or in the cellhouses. they mill about like a herd of cattle before a storm breaks. They are conscious, and their consciousness rocks the boat, dangerously.

"These cats are opposed not only by the 'authorities' but also by a great many inmates who are caught up in what must be a most painful situation—especially for the black old-timers and the black pseudo-hipsters. The convict mentality, you see, is the slave mentality magnified. And for the old-timers to see the authority of white men to rule black men being questioned by these cats is like seeing the sun rise in the west.

". . . in the meantime, what is going to happen to these young men here who might have been hewers of wood or climbers of high mountains? Well, they will wait, milling about with sparks dancing in their eyes, until the storm breaks, until the built-in contradictions of this racist, exploitative system burst through its already cracking seams."

*   *   *

Finally, I would like to express my thanks to Roberto Giammanco, whose friendship and letters are a gas, and to Gwendolyn Brooks, Sonia Sanchez, Dudley Randall, and Don L. Lee: black poets whose love and words cracked these walls.

Etheridge Knight
Indiana State Prison
October 1968

CONTENTS

Introduction
by Roberto Giammanco

"Being a man is the continuing battle of one's life; one loses a bit of manhood with every stale compromise to the authority of any power in which one does not believe. No slave should die a natural death. There is a point where caution ends and cowardice begins. Every day I am in prison I will refuse both food and water.

"My hunger is for the liberation of my people; my thirst is for the ending of oppression. I am a political prisoner, jailed for my beliefs that black people must be free. The government has taken a position true to its fascist nature. Those who they cannot convert, they must silence. This government has become the enemy of mankind.

"Death can no longer alter our path to freedom. For our people, death has been the only known exit from slavery and oppression. We must open others. Our will to live must no longer supersede our will to fight, for our fighting will determine if our race shall live.

"To desire freedom is not enough. We must move from resistance to aggression, from revolt to revolution. For every black death, there must be ten dead racist cops. For every Max Stanford and Huey Newton, there must be ten Detroits; and for every Orangeburg, there must be a Dienbienphu.

"Brothers and Sisters, and all oppressed peoples, we must prepare ourselves both mentally and physically, for the major confrontation is yet to come. We must fight. It is the people who in the final analysis make and determine history, not leaders or systems. The laws to govern us must be made by us . . . "*

This is how H. Rap Brown, a ghetto youth, a black man without power, wrote to his people when he was imprisoned still another time for being a black power spokesman. It was on February 21, 1968, the third anniversary of the assassination of Malcolm X, and Brown was in prison in New Orleans.

These are new words for a new generation which knows that it can survive only through a tough, total struggle projected into the future. They bear the unmistakable mark of a break with the traditional Negro self-image, which historically was the creation of White Power.

A black man in prison reflects the totality of the condition of his people. In the past, ruling white society could view him with pity, indifference, self-satisfaction; today it must come to terms with him.

"I'm perfectly aware that I'm in prison, that I'm a Negro, that I've been a rapist, and that I have a Higher Uneducation. I never know what significance I'm supposed to attach to these factors. But I have a suspicion that, because of these aspects of my character, 'free-normal-educated' people rather expect me to be more reserved, penitent, remorseful, and not too quick to shoot off my mouth on certain subjects. But I let them down, disappoint them, make them gape at me in a sort of stupor, as if they're thinking: 'You've got your nerve! Don't you realize that you owe a debt to society?' My answer to all such thoughts lurking in their split-level heads, crouching behind their squinting bombardier eyes, is that the blood of Vietnamese peasants has paid off all my debts; that the Vietnamese people, afflicted with a rampant disease called Yankees, through their suffer-

* *The Black Panther*, March, 1968.

ings — as opposed to the 'frustration' of fat-assed American geeks safe at home worrying over whether to have bacon, ham, or sausage with their grade-A eggs in the morning, while Vietnamese worry each morning whether the Yankees will gas them, burn them up, or blow away their humble pads in a hail of bombs — have canceled all my IOUs."*

These are the words of another black man, imprisoned for many years in the penitentiary at Folsom, California. Folsom is one of the better-known places on the map of the Afro-American: San Quentin, Harlem, Indiana State Prison, South Side, Soledad, Watts. Ghettos and prisons, inevitable steps on the road.

Like many other youths of the ghetto, Eldridge Cleaver followed an objective course of events that ended in a penitentiary. In prison he became a Black Muslim, then a follower of Malcolm X after the latter split with Elijah Muhammad, and is today one of the spokesmen of the struggle for liberation of the Afro-American.

So-called Negro criminality is neither a social phenomenon consisting of the sum total of individual events, nor is it, as the academic sociologists maintain, a manifestation of a culture of poverty or of social disintegration. Principally it is a mechanism implicit in the reality of the ghettos and the manner in which white society projects its hegemony over its outcasts.

The first step for the ghetto youth is the pure and simple rejection of the law. It is an automatic refusal anticipated by the power structure, which does everything possible to channel it into lucrative substructures that serve also as safety valves for social tensions. For the ghetto youth, the law signifies systematic and unpunished police brutality, judicial partiality, governmental indifference and civil-rights hypocrisy. The laws are made by and for store and pawnshop owners, by and for landlords and employers, by and for labor unions which stub-

---

* Eldridge Cleaver, *Soul on Ice*, McGraw-Hill Book Company, Inc., New York, 1968, p. 18.

bornly defend the guild privileges of white workmen, by and for the army which gives draft priority to the young men of the ghettos and sends them off to die in Vietnam. And those by and for whom the laws are made visualize the Negro as all brawn, a dancer, a musician, an athlete, an exotic phallic animal, in his own way exciting and potentially threatening.

For the ghetto youth, rejecting the law is one of the "facts of life." Attending school means being continually told of one's social, psychological, and human inferiority, or being persuaded to repress one's every impulse. Not attending school means never emerging from, never risking alienation from, the life of the black community. The boy of the ghetto grows up in the midst of adults who struggle, as Malcolm said, in a jungle.

Here are some teachers' reports on Harlem children.

DONALD

He has so many things going on all over the building, he's out all the time. He sells cards, works in the lunchroom; teachers invite him in to help with plants or retarded children. He's gone all the time.

ERNIE PETIT

He needs to feel some concern on the part of the school authorities. Yesterday, he took the children home to his mother's apartment at noon; they smoked cigarettes, sniffed glue, cooked pork chops and collard greens, set the curtains on fire, and cleared out leaving pools of water, to get back to school forty minutes late. I asked what they did about the water. "Nothing." Ernie's been in school a few days all semester. Now he's gone again.

CURTIS

He showed up in class last Tuesday with a stolen ten-dollar bill—it was the day after welfare checks. He got away. The children say his father beat him with a coat hanger that night, opened the top of his eye. Can't we do something?*

These same teachers report a typical episode. There was a plant in the school which, much to the sorrow of some students, died. Richard and William were sent to buy another.

RICHARD: William wanted to take the first flower he saw. Not me. You got to get one that won't die. We've got more than a flower here, we've got a plant. Had William keep guard, took my time. We paid. But the big boys come after us anyway, walking on their heels behind us. We had to run! It's this Christmas time coming. All the teen-age boys in Jefferson, they want money for their girl friends' Christmas presents. They are *laying* for you!

They gets it with knives, K55. They looking to buy her a present. Carry your money in your underwear, teacher, or in you socks! Those boys dangerous, put the knife up to you; they put it to little kids and say, Your money or your life!

— Teen-agers they break into those wine stores on the weekend. They need the money, wanta go buy those three-quarters coats that look like leather . . .

— When you steal in the dime store, he takes you in that room and beats you. But it's his business; he can do that. Either the white guy beats you or that colored guy. Dime store's almost goin out of business, they steal so much.**

The end point of the dynamic of the ghetto is the black man in prison. He is the mirror image of the condition of the Afro-American and the white society. An age-old inferiority complex, the conscious and systematic exclusion from the power structure and from social

---

*Mary F. Greene and Orletta Ryan, *The Schoolchildren: Growing Up in the Slums,* Pantheon Books, New York, 1964, pp. 127-128.
** *Ibid.,* p.60.

existence are articulated in psychological forms that must be uprooted, reversed, and replaced.

Whereas rejecting the law, as such, represents an objective condition for the ghetto youth, an automatic response, the uprooting of the Negro self-image, inculcated from birth, represents a long, revolutionary process.

"Somehow I arrived at the conclusion that, as a matter of principle, it was of paramount importance for me to have an antagonistic, ruthless attitude toward white women. The term *outlaw* appealed to me and at the time my parole date was drawing near, I considered myself to be mentally free—I was an "outlaw." I had stepped outside of the white man's law, which I repudiated with scorn and self-satisfaction. I became a law unto myself— my own legislature, my own supreme court, my own executive. At the moment I walked out of the prison gate, my feelings toward white women in general could be summed up in the following lines:

TO A WHITE GIRL

I love you
Because you're white,
Not because you're charming
Or bright.
Your whiteness
Is a silky thread
Snaking through my thoughts
In redhot patterns
Of lust and desire.

I hate you
Because you're white.
Your white meat
Is nightmare food.

> *White is*
> *The skin of Evil.*
> *You're my Moby Dick,*
> *White Witch,*
> *Symbol of the rope and hanging tree,*
> *Of the burning cross.*
> *Loving you thus*
> *And hating you so,*
> *My heart is torn in two.*
> *Crucified.*

I became a rapist. To refine my technique and *modus operandi,* I started out by practicing on black girls in the ghetto — in the black ghetto where dark and vicious deeds appear not as aberrations or deviations from the norm, but as part of the sufficiency of the Evil of a day — and when I considered myself smooth enough, I crossed the tracks and sought out white prey. I did this consciously, deliberately, willfully, methodically — though looking back I see that I was in a frantic, wild, and completely abandoned frame of mind.

"Rape was an insurrectionary act. It delighted me that I was defying and trampling upon the white man's law, upon his system of values, and that I was defiling his women — and this point, I believe, was the most satisfying to me because I was very resentful over the historical fact of how the white man has used the black woman. I felt I was getting revenge. From the site of the act of rape, consternation spreads outwardly in concentric circles. I wanted to send waves of consternation throughout the white race."*

Another step: the obsessive image of the white woman, projection of terror and racial resentment, which is internalized by and becomes a part of black men.

---

* Cleaver, *Soul on Ice*, pp. 13-14.

Again it is white society, almost like a mechanism of damnation, that speaks from the mouth of the black man, obliged to reflect his persecutor.

"And in my confusion and fear and sorrow I dived into the dope-world head first," writes George Page in one of the pieces collected in this volume. "The years of fighting my fear of the white man and the confusion of trying to live in the world of his creation are inexpressible."

The great escape offered by drugs, the wondrous world lit up by reefers and heroin, does not correspond to effete cultural or psychological needs. Drugs, here, do not reflect the frustration of the white middle class but rather the inescapable terror which flows from inferiority, from social impotence, from alienation.

Social and psychological inferiority are identical mechanisms. Comparisons with the European peasant bound to his aspiration for land ownership, his attachment to his village, family and parish, are irrelevant. The ghetto black has learned that he is not a man. It is repeated to him every day in a million ways: the highest level of unemployment, the largest group getting unemployment compensation and welfare, the group with the lowest percentage of professionals, technicians and skilled workers, those with the lowest IQ ratings in elementary and high school.

"One tactic by which the rulers of America have kept the bemused millions of Negroes in optimum subjugation has been a conscious, systematic emasculation of Negro leadership. Through an elaborate system of sanctions, rewards, penalties, and persecutions — with, more often than not, members of the black bourgeoisie acting as hatchet men — any Negro who sought leadership over the black masses and refused to become a tool of the white power structure was either cast into prison, killed, hounded out of the country, or blasted into obscurity and isolation in his own land and among his own people." *

The only leadership allowed the black masses previously was that selected by white power. Ghettos have never been permitted to express themselves through the emergence of their natural leaders; the cat on the street sees in this another clear proof of his inferiority, of his social impotence.

"The murder of Malcolm X," writes Eldridge Cleaver, "the exile of Robert F. Williams, who was forced to flee to Cuba with the combined terrors of the FBI and the minions of Southern justice snapping at his heels, and the exile of the late W. E. B. DuBois, who, in the sunset of his valiant life, made three symbolic gestures as a final legacy to his people (renouncing his American citizenship, 'returning' to Africa to become a citizen of Ghana, and cursing capitalism while extolling communism as the hope of the future)—these events on the one hand, and on the other hand the award of a Nobel Prize to Martin Luther King and the inflation of his image to that of an international hero, bear witness to the historical fact that the only Negro Americans allowed to attain national or international fame have been the puppets and lackeys of the white power structure—and entertainers and athletes." **

The black man in prison is the sum total of all of these historical privations, more concentrated for the ghetto inhabitant caught up in a system which regards him as a model of maladjustment, prone to what white society's racial prejudice lists under the headings of degeneration, abnormal behavior and individual disintegration.

These criteria of white psychology are collapsing one by one. The mental structure of the white middle class is conditioned by the idea of the Negro's inferiority,

---

* *Ibid.*, p. 87.
** *Ibid.*

by his threatening presence as the potential predator on white women, by the opportunity for using violence against blacks without fear of punishment. In its present state, white society is not prepared to recognize the Afro-American as a man; it can do so neither from the objective point of view of its economic interests, nor at the level of subjective comprehension. The Italians of Cicero and Newark, the Poles of Milwaukee and Hamtramck, the Jews of Brooklyn, have been the last to "arrive" at the middle-class scale of values and are, therefore, the most ferocious and least sophisticated racists.

Suburbia, the oldest member of that blessed middle class, closest to the founts of its wealth, views the ghetto Negro as a threat to that traditional structure of ruling class values which makes possible suburban living, the monopoly of degrees from the "right" kind of college, the right kind of jobs, and intermediate forms of power in the power structure.

This traditional psychological structure of the middle class worked as long as the Afro-American was unaware of the international nexus of the mechanisms of exploitation and racism, as long as his only recourses were Christian resignation or the return to Africa. Making exception for those individual cases of maladjustment, for those fallen by the wayside through extreme poverty or vice, the Negro fulfilled a precise role, definable, foreseeable and, more significantly, one that symbolized all that the middle class unconsciously detested (particularly in itself, in its own daily behavior), even in its own ethico-religious ideals.

The white man's virility was never threatened because, if a minority of Negroes behaved instinctively, it was always possible to trace the roots of this behavior to their natural state of *infantility*, whereas the Negro "majority" followed, for good or ill, Christian principles. The security of the power structure corresponded to the logic of its rationalization.

Once the black man realizes that he goes to prison

first because he is black and then because he breaks the law, that he breaks the law because being black signifies being outside the law, that his subjective condition is the hinge upon which white exploitation revolves, in that moment the relationship is reversed.

The insecurity of the power structure once the phase of integration — civil rights — is over and once the ghetto's political consciousness has been awakened, goes hand in hand with the collapse of the society's traditional psychological *points of reference.* The dynamics of the society have been moving in this direction for a long time, and at this point the question of power is one with that of being recognized as men. The black man rejects white society's "right" to define him, to teach him to know himself as a black man, to project his future. The struggle for liberation has begun.

This book is a collection of Etheridge Knight's writings and writings of other prisoners sent to me by and through him. They are testimonies of the life of black prisoners, almost all of them in the Indiana penitentiary. Above all, they are clinical case histories of a consciously lived condition by protagonists and victims at different levels of understanding, criticism, and sensibility. They are pages brimming with "discoveries" happily lacking in literary echoes, turbulent in their dramatic search for the external and internal enemy.

In their skeletal style, composed of concrete imagery, or comparisons which our ruling culture considers banal (but which successive waves of "lovers of the common people" have co-opted for their own esthetic-moralistic gratification), these pages constitute an overwhelming denunciation of racism and colonialism, not only as practiced by white society, but also as they were and are accepted by Negroes.

A long procession of characters files before us. There is the old man imprisoned for life who sees his city again after twenty-four years; the rebellious young man who fights like an ancient warrior against pitiless prison repression: Charles Baker, a lifer, twenty-three years old, who, like Malcolm, Eldridge Cleaver and many others, finds in the teachings of the Black Muslims a way to begin his struggle for freedom.

"I don't believe that there is a God in existence . . . because I can't see God existing and seeing the black man be misused as he is today throughout the world. I can't see this, and so I can't accept Islam. If anything, I accept the black man as being a god, each being a god. But I do accept the teaching of Islam that the white man is the devil because I think the white man has proved himself to be the devil."

There is William Healy, a young white boy from a middle class family, who is an example of the reverse side of the coin of racism. He recounts the stages of his religious experience, his obedience to the divinity that was nothing more than the symbol of real and psychological subordination inflicted upon him by society.

"Once the full implication and weight of my sentence crashed into my consciousness, with a realization more and more creeping in that prison was far from pleasant, the prayers, rank with human bargaining and irreverence, began to fall from my lips: 'Oh, if only you would cut me loose . . . ' And I also turned to that beautiful prayer first recited by St. Bernard in honor of the Blessed Virgin, the *Memorare.* It opens: 'Remember, O most gracious Virgin Mary, that never was it known that anyone who fled to thy protection, implored thy help and sought thine intercession, was left unaided . . .

"This insipid fervor was used to stoke the fires of hope, and it lasted three nights as I religiously recited the prayer again and again; but repetition also to give up ever praying again, to find in rejection a new justification . . . I felt more like a Christian inside the lion than in the lion's den; for when the inner flame flickered in anguish and loneliness, prayer was extinguished."

"Whitey" has modeled his prisons as a place meant to

destroy any interest in life. The weaker prisoners succumb to an internalized sense of guilt which seals
their sense of exclusion, while in stronger subjects the
necessity to resist or adapt themselves to a strict, formal
discipline destroys in them any future aspirations. Prison confirms their exclusion, social annihilation, and
permanent inferiority.

"Yet the great majority of prisoners endure, with a
proud, unyielding spirit that will not bend to prison:
men who are capable in one moment of an act of tremendous human charity toward another man they hardly
know — and in the same instant recipients or purveyors
of vicious cruelty."

The power structure is reduced to the essential, ex-
emplified. Skin color means less than on the outside, but
it conserves all of its sexual mystique, distorted as the
white collective pathology wills it. In the prison world,
the competitive relationship outside manifests itself at
primary levels, pregnant with cruelty. The law of prison
carries to its final and merciless logic the principle of
"every man for himself," thereby splitting any form of
solidarity. The system of rewards and punishments is
so structured that it keeps the prisoners divided among
themselves and, more significantly, pits one against
another. Any individual advantage: temporary freedom,
brief permission in the courtyard, being assigned a
light workload, are concessions made to certain individuals to the exclusion of the others.

The competititon is destructive, all within regulations
which do not even define the limits of power, but analyze,
with Byzantine ferocity, every conceivable motion, every
foreseeable and unforeseeable action of the prisoners.
Even if skin color has secondary importance in the
code of survival within the prison, the racism of white
society is clearly reflected in the mechanism of the authoritarian prison power structure.

Once the black man is freed, he not only shares the

destiny of all ex-prisoners, but finds the entire mechanism of exclusion completely intact.

"Finally," writes Etheridge Knight in "Inside These Walls," "when a man *is* paroled, he is given $15 in cash and a new suit of clothes (out of style) by the state. And most men leaving prison have nothing on which to rely until they can draw a paycheck. (During the years in prison he has earned an average of ten cents a day. A bar of soap costs twenty cents, in prison.)

"Ninety-nine times out of a hundred, a man leaving prison is going to work on a blue-collar job, so the new suit of clothes is without utility. The fifteen dollars will hardly provide him with a place to stay — to say nothing of the personal necessities: work clothes, razor and toothbrush, etc. Because of all this, a man who has a wife or relatives on whom he must rely is from the outset put into an embarrassing, self-demeaning position. A man who has no wife or close relatives is forced to seek out old friends, usually those in an environment which quickly shoves him back into criminal activities.

"Small wonder then that 75 per cent of all ex-convicts return to crime . . ."

Then there are the innocent, that is, those whom the prisoners themselves, beyond all doubt, have recognized as innocent. They are the men whom the judicial juggernaut throws behind bars merely because it was necessary to condemn someone for a serious crime and was easier and safer to incriminate a black man. In Etheridge Knight's "The Innocents," this process is described. The Afro-American, poor and with a prison record for minor offenses, is, though innocent, found guilty. He has neither means nor social power to vindicate himself, so he remains in prison despite the fact that "theoretically" he could be freed by an act of clemency, a retrial, or any number of legal loopholes. On the other hand, even if he were freed, do not the statistics reveal that over 70 per cent of ex-prisoners return to jail?

Clarence Harris' one-act play, "The Trip," presents

an almost orgiastic, hallucinatory dimension of black rebellion. A Zulu warrior, who kills two policemen, symbolizes the terror of the unexpected. All of the points of reference of the system are reversed when the reactions of black people no longer follow the established lines of conduct. Guerrilla warfare is the mechanism of this short theatrical work.

In "A Time To Mourn" by Etheridge Knight, we find at attempt to express, in the broken and stuttering language of sorrow, in the contrast between real participation and conventional "suffering," the need for solitude as the prisoner's only means of defense. Contacts with the outside world must be reevaluated, must be viewed with detachment, given the necessity of existence without the mediation of affection. But this amputation, necessitated by circumstance, is also great strength, because it destroys self-pity, *victimismo*.

Many of these pages alternate the toughness of a dearly bought self-sufficiency with nostalgic, idealized recollections of the past.

But the most significant aspect of the experiences recorded in these documents lies in the pride manifested against repression and in unflinching, lucid self-criticism. A new human dimension emerges from these pages. That they were written in prison is no longer significant: much is valid for all ghettos, for the oppressed of all countries, for all men who need to discover or rediscover the image of the enemy.

These pages, transcribed by the Negro poet Etheridge Knight during his long imprisonment, frequently seem primitively, vaguely conceived, but only on the level of expression. The basic ideas were and are extremely clear, increasingly clear.

We face, not the damnation of the few, an existential problem which might be resolved through "pardon," but rational, deaf, inhuman, efficient violence, institutionalized violence. The pages record the landmarks along the obligatory path of those who are its victims.

Within the prison walls there are no alternatives, because even before, in the ghettos, there were none.

The condition of the black man is the full realization of institutionalized violence and prefigures all others. Skin color is still very important: for the white man there still remain formal psychological alternatives, because "after all there are always the Negroes."

In one of his letters, one of the contributors asked me to make clear that the writings are the product of those "who have learned to know Whitey." That is, those who discover that falsehood and violence are not subjective, accidental phenomena, but rather the objective and permanent dimension of the power structure and the false alternatives it presents.

The struggle for liberty for which the pages of this collection were written, their cost in suffering, would be in vain if we cannot hope that they will be read and pondered by all those who refuse to be accomplices of institutionalized violence. The words of these black prisoners, of these sons of the ghetto, cannot remain interesting but foreign to those who, in diverse circumstances, are learning to recognize *Whitey* throughout the world.

In the spirit of the pages that follow, I dedicate this book to all those who fight against the existence of ghettos, more or less visible, more or less hallucinatory, which the power structure creates and administers everywhere.

Roberto Giammanco
Rome
May, 1968

Testament

by David Flournoy

I am twenty-four years old, and I am black. I am serving four sentences: life, 10-25 years, 2-21 years, and 1-5 years, for kidnap, robbery, rape, and attempted escape respectively, and as I understand it all these charges stem from the same incident. I am not going to talk about my crimes, nor about my guilt or innocence. I am going to talk about here in this prison, after I fill you in on a little of my background. (Knight suggested that I also talk about what I think the future holds for me and for other boys like me; but how in the hell do I know?)

I come from a large family in the Deep South, although shortly after I was born we moved north of the Mason and Dixon Line to a little town where the Mississippi and Ohio rivers meet. It was an area mixed with Northerners and Southerners and their ways of living. Black people had little shanties on the north and east sides of town. The memories of my early years are nothing. I can recall only a very few times that I was what you would call happy or contented. It has always been for me like when I used to go swimming and get caught in the cross-currents of the two rivers meeting.

It seems to me that I have always been fighting. I'm a little guy and I learned early that in order for me

to win I had to get the first punch in. And I really
don't like to fight; I just grew into it like I grew into
manhood. I finally made it through high school and
split town soon afterward. I couldn't wait to get away.
Two of my buddies and I stole a car and we lit out,
robbing, drinking, and balling. As I said before, I've
been fighting all my life. When me and my buddies
weren't fighting somebody from our end of town, we
would go peckerwood hunting, hoping to find some
white boys our age to beat up. We won most of the
time, but sometimes we lost. But until we left home
we had never had the nerve to fight any grown-up
white man. After the first time it was easy. Our specialty
was bopping the whiteys that came to the colored sections of towns looking for women. We fought and robbed
and balled for six months and all the time it was like
I was outside of me or like I was saying no, no to
myself.

And then I fell and came here. Before that though,
there was jail which wasn't too bad because my two
buddies were still with me, but after the trial they were
sent to the reformatory and I was sent here because
I got life and they don't send guys with life to the
reformatory even if they're ten years old. When I hit
quarantine, I was ready for anything. I had heard
the tales. I was just waiting to be shackled to some
wall or be put into some dungeon and given a whip-
lashing. But nothing happened, and quarantine was
pretty cool. My folks came to see me for the first time—
it wouldn't have done any good if they had come to
the trial cause nobody's got any money anyways. Well,
finally I was let out in general population, and then
the trouble started.

Like I said, I had heard the talk, plus I've always
read a lot, so I knew what to expect in a way, and
I had made up my mind that the first time some guy
approached me about sex that I was going to get me

another life sentence. I saw no other way. I mean, I couldn't go running to the officials 'cause in a way it's better to be a punk than a rat when you got to live in this joint for years and years. And anyway, what could the officials do? Nothing but lock you up or lock the guy up for a few months, and then when the guy get out you still got trouble on your hands. Maybe more trouble. So I figured that at the first sign of that sex jive I had better do something quick and definite and permanent, and I got me a knife. But I didn't have to use it. I was lucky. There were other young black cats here and I hung out with them and nobody mentioned that kind of stuff to them 'cause if he did we'd stomp him. The young white boys, some of them are stupid, all they'd have to do is run together and then they wouldn't have to put up with that jive. But to tell the truth, there's no brutality here, no muscle. Those guys just go for candy or cigarettes.

The sex thing was solved but I still got into a lot of trouble and probably still will. I guess I've always been crazy or else all the fighting and the way I've been acting most of my life wouldn't make any sense.

Sometimes I get scared, I mean, everything is nothing, nothing. Sometimes I feel like I want to get inside somebody else, then again I don't. I mean, I listen to the radio and read the papers and, shit, everybody's crazy out there too. I mean, it ain't nothing. Things're as tight out there in the world as they are in here, and in here ain't nothing. But something's got to give. I mean, I want to live, but even to die wouldn't be so bad, but it would be a bitch to die in here. Prison is a bitch. So now I follow the rules, it still ain't nothing. But I'll make it, I mean, something will happen sooner or later, cause I now *know* that all this shit ain't right— I mean, I know that what happened to me and what I did was not me.

Everywhere you look you hear whitey running down

his jive. It's the same soup, just warmed over. He still ain't going to raise up off the black man, even in here he ain't raised up. In the streets a colored guy is last to be hired and the first to be fired; in here, he's the last one to make a parole and the first one to be denied. I mean, it ain't nothing.

So I go to my job and eat and sleep. I read and listen and get hip. And something's going to break, I guess.

Testament

by Louis J. Bean

I was thirteen years old when I first encountered the protectors of society and when I first learned what it really meant to be poor in a society that measures a man more or less by his wealth. I had run away from home and left town with a carnival that had completed its week's stand in Dayton, Ohio. I began by working at odd jobs, such as putting up and tearing down tents and concession stands. I liked the excitement and hustle of the carnival, and soon I had graduated to being a ticket seller at one of the several burlesque shows. I soon became wise to the fact that I could make ten to fifteen dollars extra every night if I would cooperate with the ticket taker, who would give me a handful of tickets that could be resold and we would split the profits.

I worked on this job for a couple of months, until the manager saw the ticket taker shove me a fistful of tickets which had just been deposited in the ticket-taker's box. First the manager threatened to knock my head off, then he decided to call the sheriff. While he went to the office trailer to call the cops, I took what money I had in the money box and went to the highway and hitched a ride into town. I was arrested just outside the city limits by a deputy sheriff. He promptly clamped the long arms of the law on

my wrists and carted me off to the city's juvenile
center. I was there eleven days before they released
me to my mother, who immediately went into her
act and spanked and screamed at me until I promised that I would never do anything again. The officials
kept my money, even the money that was really mine.

I was released to my mother and was back in Dayton that evening. I was reenrolled in the parochial
school and was doing all right until about a year
later when a buddy of mine decided that he wanted
to join the navy and forged his birth certificate. I
did the same, and we wound up in the Great Lakes
Naval Training Center in the state of Illinois.

We soon tired of the rough training program and
we decided to go over the back fence and enjoy a little
freedom. We enjoyed our freedom and were in jail
in Hot Springs, Arkansas, exactly ten days later.
We had been arrested for speeding in a car that we
had stolen in Chicago the previous day. The FBI
charged my buddy and me with taking a stolen vehicle
across the state line, and I received a three-year sentence in the federal reformatory and an undesirable
discharge from the navy.

After my release from the federal pen, I roamed
around my hometown for a few months and finally
took a job in a war plant that made, of all things,
machine guns. For some reason the steady work bugged
me, so after about three months I quit the job and
started driving stolen cars from one town to another
for a friend of mine who I had met while in the federal
pen. I made good money for the chances I took; I
received $250 for each car I delivered no matter
what the distance.

This went on for about seven months, until I was
stopped one day in a roadblock that had been set
up because a bank had been robbed in the area. The
cops at the roadblock asked for my driver's license

and auto registration, which I, of course, didn't have. So I was arrested on some kind of charge that slips my mind at the present time. The car was checked out, and me also. I was taken to jail and in due time I was sentenced to five years.

I did every day of the five years because I could not stay out of trouble. If you're seventeen you get into a lot of fights in prison. I was put in the hole several times for fighting, making booze, and gambling.

When I was finally released from the federal prison again, I had made up my mind that I would get a job and settle down and try the so-called good life, but I soon found out that it takes money for the good life as well as for the bad life. About nine months later I ran into an old buddy that I had done time with and he had some very good ideas, at least they seemed so at the time. We started pulling stickups. One night after a drugstore holdup, my buddy gave me my first shot of narcotics. I started taking cocaine whenever we had a job to pull because I felt that I could carry my part of the job better and faster. But one day I was shot in the leg while robbing a super-market and was caught hobbling down an alley a couple of blocks away. I was taken back to the store and identified by the clerks. I was sentenced to ten years for this job, but I appealed the sentence and was granted bond. While out on bond I was stopped by a state trooper for speeding. I knew that if I was taken to jail I would forfeit my bond.

I have almost always carried a pistol of some sort. So I pulled it and told the state trooper to turn his back to me and raise his hands. I jumped into my car and drove about three miles down the road and right smack into a roadblock that the trooper had called in for.

For that I received another ten years. So I'm now doing two ten-flat sentences which means that I will have to do six years and eight months for each sentence.

For the past few years I have often lain on my bunk
and wondered what makes a man such a fool when
he knows deep down in his heart that he can't get away
with a lot of things. Yet he goes right on trying when
he really doesn't want to. The guy who wrote this
poem must have been talking about people like me:

> There's a race of men that don't fit in,
> A race that can't stay still;
> So they break the hearts of kith and kin;
> And roam the world at will.
>
> They range the field and they rove the flood,
> And they climb the mountain crest.
> Theirs is the curse of the Gypsy blood,
> And they don't know how to rest.
>
> If they just went straight they might go far;
> They are strong and brave and true;
> But they are always tired of the things that are,
> And they want the strange and new.

Interview of Charles W. Baker
by Charles W. Baker*

First of all I would like to state that I would like for you to excuse my hesitation in answering the questions. . . uh. . . I will start with the first one.

The first one says, "Tell me something about yourself and your family." First of all I would like to start with myself: My name is Charles Wesley Baker, and I'm twenty-three years old. I am in this institution now for four years, since I was nineteen. I was convicted out of South Bend, Indiana, and I'm doing a life sentence for murder in the commission of a robbery.

Uh. . . when I first came to this institution I participated in a few things: I participated in boxing — I guess I participated in boxing for an outlet — I participated in boxing cause I was bored, I was mad, and this was a way of escaping, and so, I started boxing; and, also I participated in education; I felt that this was a necessity, that this was something that I had to do for myself, is to try to educate myself.

And also, I came in contact with Islam since I've been in this institution, and I feel that this is one of the things that woke me up to recognize and to face reality. To see what exists. . . uh. . . within my surroundings. When I came into this institution, by me being mad, angry at society, and plus that, feeling that I had got an injustice, I accepted the. . . uh. . . teachings of Islam.

---

*This is a transcript of a tape recording made by Charles W. Baker, alone in his cell, in reply to a written list of questions.

And my reasons for accepting the teachings of Islam are because I recognized from the teachings of Islam that this white man was the devil, I recognized from the teachings of Islam that this white man had deceived the black man, had misled the black man, had indoctrinated the black man, had trained the black man to think — had conditioned his way of thinking. And this. . . when the teachings of Islam — when I first heard the teachings of Islam, it was something new, it was something that I had never heard before and. . . it was something that I wanted to think but didn't know how to think it. . . Uh. . . the teachings of Islam told me that the white man was the devil, it told me that the white man had stole the black man from the continent of Africa, had murdered him millions by millions, and after I see this racial turmoil in this society, after I think about how my mother and father have been. . . uh. . . victimized, after I think about myself, then the teachings of Islam becomes a lot of truth to me. I accepted it; and, as a matter of fact, even today, I still accept a great deal of the teachings of the Honorable Elijah Muhammad. Uh. . . I will speak of this later on.

Uh. . . I would also like to speak of how Islam drove me into education. When I first came in here, I didn't have any knowledge of myself, uh. . . I didn't have any knowledge of my black ancestry, and so, in order for one to comprehend, he must have a foundation, and so this is what I had to do: I had to build me a foundation. And so I went to school. I went to school with the intentions that I would have to. . . uh. . . reeducate myself; I had to improve myself, I had to make myself into what I wanted to be, and I had to tear down what this white man had built up within me. And so this was my basic reason for going back to school. Uh. . . I don't wanna stray too much off these questions here. I would like to answer each one of them. And I hope you got a pretty good idea of me. As for my parents, they are just plain black people who work hard, like most black people, and who get messed over, like most black people.

Uh. . . I would like to state the second question. It says, "Tell me how you feel being in the penitentiary with a life sentence." Well, I know one thing: I don't feel too good, although this is something that I have to bear along with. Uh. . . it say, also, "Tell me how you feel about sex, and the rules, and the officials of the institution."

Uh. . . I have a whole lot of hidden animosity in me for this system, I have a whole lot of hidden animosity for the officials of this institution; and as far as the rules are concerned, uh. . . they are something which I have to abide by. There are some things which I got to go along with, for the benefit of myself. . . uh. . . although I have to admit that I haven't been going along with them. I have tried to rebel against the rules, I have tried to oppose the officers of the institution, but I see that all this is detrimental to me, and all this is keeping me. . . uh. . . uh. . . from reaching some of my goals. And so, I recognize now the fact that I have to go along with the rules of the institution. . . uh, whether I like it or not. . . uh. . . as long as they don't go against something that I definitely know, something that presses me into a ball.

I would like to skip over a few of these questions [referring to sex] and go down to: "When you first came here, you embraced Islam. Tell me what you thought of it then, and what you think of it now."

Uh . . . I think I answered the question of why I embraced Islam . . . and what do I think of it now? Uh, I think of Islam as being a religion, just like any other religion. . . uh. . . waiting. . . uh. . . praying and hoping that some supernatural power will change what is happening and what is reality. I can't go along with that part of it, I can't follow Elijah Muhammad, because I don't believe black people should wait for God to save them—whether it's a Black Allah or a white Jesus. I believe the time is now; I believe we have to put forth effort; I believe we have to make the change occur ourselves. I don't believe that there is a God in existence. . . because I can't see God existing and seeing the black man be misused as he is today throughout the world. I can't see this, and so I can't accept Islam. If anything, I accept the black man as being a god, each being a god. But I do accept the teaching of Islam that the white man is the devil because I think the white man has proved himself to be the devil.

Now, I would like to go up to the question, "Tell me what you think about the civil rights movement."

See, I could separate the civil rights movement into two or three classes. You have the militant class and you have a what you would call the mild class, which is the nonviolent, and you also have a class that is on the religious kick, you know?—they don't wanna put forth no effort because they think that there is a pie in the sky. And there are those who feel as I do—that in order to obtain, you must take. And what we would be taking is that which is rightfully ours, and that is freedom, freedom as human beings. . . uh. . . .

And also, there are those who are trying to pacify. . . uh. . . uh. . . like Martin Luther King, who says that he will love the white man into submission. And, uh, see, this is something that is a waste of time. We got to do the same thing the white man has done—we got to take. The white man came to this country and killed millions and millions of Indians; he went on the continent of Africa and stole millions and millions of black men and brought them over here for slavery. He killed, robbed, stole, and so this country was established upon this violence. I know one thing—I recognize one thing: that anytime a person is a master within a certain field that this is the field that you cannot fight him in; and so, we must. . . we must recognize the white man as being a militant type of individual, and not meet him with his own type of militancy but with a type that will equalize his power. We must recognize this. . .

I remember one time I was reading about the Turks. Uh. . . at one time they were great warriors who kept the white man on the continent of Europe for thousands and thousands of years; and today I look. . . I look at the Turks as being farmers. And so this just shows you that time creates the individual, and I think that the black man through the conditions that he has lived under is being created into a race of warriors. In fact, I look at the black man as being a warrior now because time creates, conditions create. . . the same way as the white man was created to invade other countries because of his location, because of his poor income in Europe, and the beginning of his factories. It was a means of survival, a means of convenience, and a particular something in time, that caused the white man to attack other countries and invade them. The circumstances and conditions created him into what he is. And this is the same thing that this society has done to the black man.

And we. . . this question of a. . . of a. . . Martin Luther King. What do I think of Martin Luther King? He's a tom. Roy Wilkins' a tom. And what do I think of Malcolm X? He was created by a racist society. As a matter of fact, I love Malcolm X, Stokely Carmichael, and Rap Brown. And as soon as Stokely and Rap are assassinated like Malcolm was, there will be other Stokelys and Raps who will snatch the covers off the white man. Because the problem exists; and the times created these cats, and the conditions created them. And so there will always be somebody who will tell the truth that we all already know, until the white man acts right. And guys like Martin Luther King — he's behind. Unless he just plain sold out somebody. And this is probably the case. You know, he. . . he's used to the white man's culture, he's accepted the white man's way of life. . .

Uh. . . I would like to make an attempt to answer this question: "Do you think the black man will ever overcome? If so, how? If not, why?"

We have to take into consideration that this country is a powerful country. This country has a high economic power; it has. . . it is. . . uh. . . it has a great military force. . . and the black man is the minority and, plus that, the black man is separated. He's not united, and. . . to answer this question would be to. . . it's hard to see the black man forcing this government to change, and really, this is the only way that the black man will overcome; because as long as there, as long as he plans on getting his rights through the legislature, I think he's chasing moonbeams. I. . . uh. . . heard Malcolm once state — he said you can change the laws, you know? You can change the laws, but yet and still this don't stop the person's way of thinking. Uh. . . and see, society is. . . this is a racist society, the white man is prejudiced against the black man, the white man opposes the black man. . . and. . . and. . . Stokely Carmichael once gave a speech when the hippies suggested that they wanted to help in the civil rights movement. . . uh, and Stokely told them, Yeah, you can help. . . uh. . . he said, When the policemen come in the black neighborhoods and attack and start beating and shooting and siccing their dogs on people. . . he said, You can run out and throw roses, you know? Well, this is the same thing. . . the white man. . . well, there are some who say that they want to help the black man, but. . . uh. . . what are they gonna do? Pick up arms and try to overthrow this government so that the black man gets his rights?

And so this is a black man's problem, and the black man is the one who's got to fight his battle in order to obtain equality, in order to obtain social stature, in order to obtain pride, in order to obtain. . . uh. . .political stature. He has got to. . . uh. . . In order for there to be a change, in order for the black man to overcome this, he has got to bring about a change in this system. And if this system remains the same, the black man will never be considered as a human being. He will never be judged by his qualities, he will never be judged as an individual. He will always be judged as black — the white man's conception of black: nonhuman. Uh, and as long as the brother realizes this, and until those who are not united recognize the fact that he. . . this society will exist just the way it is as long as the white man has the power structure. . . And so. . . uh. . . uh. . . I don't know how to answer this question. . . I don't see no way that the black man can change this government or this white man; I mean, I just ain't that smart. The only thing I can suggest . . . [Pause, then long string of obscenities followed by nervous laughter.]

After giving this a little more thought I have to restate myself on this question about do I think the black man will overcome. Uh . . . yes, there is a possibility; this is a possibility, and the possibility is separation. I think the onliest way that the black man will accomplish his rights as a human being, I think that the way a black man will get equality is through separation. I think that the black man needs to establish his own government, establish his own rules, make his own patents. In order to do this, we must have unity, we must all get together.

I mean, we . . . can overcome, if we really want to. And I think what the black man is doing today is that he is trying to prove to himself that they really do want to overcome; he participates in these civil rights, he's showing the white man that he disapproves of his conditions, he disapproves of being a second-class citizen, he disapproves of what he has been through, his misusement, uh, and the black man as a whole, uh, opposes this system. He opposes the white man, uh, regardless of how fast he shuffles his feet, you know? Uh, he dislikes the misusement that he has received, he dislikes the misusement that his people has received. Uh, and so, the onliest way the black man can become free of all this is to separate from it. And this here is what the Honorable Elijah Muhammad has suggested, but the onliest thing wrong with that is he is waiting for Allah to bring about the separation. And I don't think that there is too much sincerity in what the Honorable Elijah Muhammad is asking for, simply for the reason that he is asking something that has already been asked for and that has already been denied. Uh, DuBois asked for it, Marcus Garvey asked for it, and all this was denied; and so, I think that the Honorable Elijah Muhammad is asking for something that he knows he can't get by asking. We're gonna have to take it.

See, I know one thing. . . I recognize one thing. They are gonna have to do one of two things to the black man if he keeps opposing this system, if riots keep breaking out. The white man has got to give the black man what he is asking for, or the white man has got to kill the black man. . . as he did the Indians. These are the onliest two things the white man would do if the black man pressured him enough — and I don't mean by peaceful demonstrations — so that he would, uh, be under a demand. He ain't gonna give us equality — he can't under this system if he wanted to, and he damned sure ain't gonna change his system of his own free will.

To change this man's system takes revolution, and I wish that I was a part of it. I wish that I had my-

self together where that I could play some part, and
probably in the future if I keep trying, and keep thinking the way that I think, then I believe that I will,
uh, accomplish this. Some kind of way, I believe that
I will become a part of it. I will play my part in help-
ing to obtain what rightfully belongs to the black man:
freedom. And I'll probably die doing this, but it don't
matter. Cause I'm already dead in here.

Testament
by Clarence Harris

I was born in Mississippi, but my father and mother, being young and the parents of two children, a girl and boy, decided to escape to the promised land. They heard that there were golden opportunities in Memphis, Tennessee, and so they went there. My father acquired a skill as a house painter. His salary was $12 a week. My mother became a housekeeper at $6 a week. We lived in a clapboard shack with an outside toilet. The house set upon four tiers of bricks; inside we had oil lamps, coal stove, and no running water. I spent my time wandering the unpaved streets or playing in our packed-clay yard. I had an old dog, and together we played games of Caucasian heroes and villains. Funny now, as I look back, the villains were always darker than the heroes, with thick mustaches like my father wore, and almost always they were dressed in black clothes. I never realized that I was playing the villain in a much larger and serious game: that of emulation which had been passed on to me in my parents' ignorance and fear.

In the beginning I had very little contact with the white man. However, one particular incident sticks out in my mind even now. A white man, speeding through our street, ran over my dog. I screamed and the man stopped. My dad came out of the house to calm me down and to talk to the man, and that's when I discovered that men were different because of their skin color. The white man told my father: "Nigger, it should have been that little nigger there instead of the dog. You should've kept them both out of the street. And don't you ask me nothing about that dog!" My father shivered, and retreated with me into the house. We never mentioned the incident again. But from that time on I was taught that the white man was king and was to be treated as such; I learned that they were to be idolized, feared, catered to, and also to be emulated as much as possible without stepping out of your place.

Not long after that we prepared to move to another promised land, further North, where we would really be saved. The new state that we were moving to had been a dream, but soon after we arrived there, the bubble burst. The Northern promised land was only a larger plantation with buildings instead of fields. There were more white overseers and exploiters, and even though you didn't come under the domination of one man, you came under the rule of all white men; though they wouldn't physically hold you or punish you, the police were still their legal fist to hold you in line. Still, there were more subtle boundary lines, and the cruelest thing of all was their paternalism.

So I became a part of the black environment in the North that had a smattering of white middle-class bourgeois values, but I couldn't handle the unreality of trying to be white. And I took to the streets. There, we had our own thing, our own language, our own special walks, our hipness and our soul, which we attributed to heart and toughness, and the ability to survive. We wanted to be kings, too, but not kings of rats. By now, I had quit school, and I knew what was happening with whitey.

My father, and others like him, was told to vote for whoever the power structure wanted him to, or no jobs could be had. And those who had jobs were paying taxes for inferior schools, no garbage pickups, no police protection, and on and on and on. So I gave up and withdrew from the whole scene. Why should I follow the rules and conduct of such a hypocritical society? Naturally I ran head on into white power: the police. And eventually I came to prison.

In prison I began to think. I saw myself for what I was, which is completely different from what I am. I saw myself as what whitey had made me, which is completely different from what I am, and I saw society as it really is for making me what I was. And knowing all this, how can I be expected to accept this society that has tried to kill me, or its religion that makes a fool out of any black man.

And prison here is nothing but a smaller version of what's happening outside. There is just as much racism here, both openly and under cover, and just like on the outside, nothing is ever done about it but talk. I've been thinking. All this talking and protesting is just another one of whitey's trick bags, because when you protest and demonstrate and all the rest, it is understood that you believe that the people you're protesting to are really fair and honest and that once you make them see, then they'll apologize and take their feet off your neck. But once that belief fades and protesting ends, then revolution begins. And the belief is fading fast.

Another Day Coming
by William Healy

That I have fallen upon hard times is reflected by this
address so I will refer to my home only as Q1, a non-
descript dwelling of little distinction except being the
first of thirty-four cells located on the flag or ground
floor range in D-cellhouse.

Yet now I am hesitant to say anything more about
prison because I feel unequal to the task of explain-
ing my imprisonment in order that another might glean
from this telling an understanding of the universal
encounter with penitentiary life.

What word is there that can duplicate the prison
experience? Or reproduce the feeling a man has of being
swallowed up by the earth; of being removed from the
rolls of the living, yet knowing there is no defense
against this feeling—nothing he can take to cure the
malady caused by his displacement? How is it possible
then for me to write about it? Being aware at the beginning of the difficulty of the chore does not quicken by
eagerness to begin.

So now I am confined to this cramped cubicle, just
large enough to die in, thinking mean thoughts about
nothing in particular, because in prison there is nothing
much to think about. My meanness is scattered all
about the cell: Sliding off a prison cot, piled high in
corners, my accumulation grows to resemble a World

War II garage waiting for a paper-collection drive to end. The notes, papers and related trivia are being assembled for this brief article, for the books that I will never write but continue to add random thoughts to until the time runs out for writing them. Sometimes I don't pray as hard for freedom as I curse inwardly for more space.

Funny now that I should. be thinking about prayer — the last time I tried was shortly after my arrival, with the first taste of prison embittering my thoughts, when there was still time left to make a legal maneuver for release.

Although my life had been one continuous expression of despair, coming to prison seemed like a more painful escape in the beginning. Especially when my incorrigible attitude towards freedom was fully matured and strengthened considerably by the use I had made of the mobility which is inherent in any free society. To make an adjustment to prison, therefore, with all of its unpleasant trappings, was not something easily managed; it was a forced exchange, the antithesis of freedom found in the prison word "institutionalize."

Once the full implication and weight of my sentence crashed into my consciousness, with a realization more and more creeping in that prison was far from pleasant, the prayers, rank with human bargaining and irreverence, began to fall from my lips: "Oh, if only you would cut me loose. . ." And I also turned to that beautiful prayer first recited by St. Bernard in honor of the Blessed Virgin, the *Memorare.* It opens: "Remember, O most gracious Virgin Mary, that never was it known that anyone who fled to thy protection, implored thy help and sought thine intercession, was left unaided. . ."

This insipid fervor was used to stoke the fires of hope, and it lasted three nights as I religiously recited the prayer again and again; but repetition also to give up ever praying again, to find in rejection a new justification. . . I felt more like a Christian inside the lion than in the lion's den; for when the inner flame flickered in anguish and loneliness, prayer was extinguished.

There is more to prayer than supplication; I can recall the advice given to me by a priest ("I don't seem to pray well, father."), who urged me to pray in thanksgiving for blessings which I'd received, in adoration and, often, penitently to beg forgiveness. In this respect I know that I didn't pray then; I know that I haven't prayed like this for a very long time.

So this is prison! Its storied existence is a legend commercialized by book and film, a fictitious narrative depicting prison as a place full of men hard and calloused beyond belief, who have committed acts against a society which, in turn, has sentenced them to this place where a man's life is given up to serving time.

Yet prison's self-image is perpetuated not by the men lodged in penal institutions (though many men have died here because of it, believing in the legend), but through an atmosphere which demands the continuation of both guilt and punishment. The great tragedy of our penal system, also its interior weakness, is its promise to be always indifferent, never conferring upon an individual the needed conditional absolution—that an adjustment within his life, in terms he understands and wants, might be tried through programs that are designed for his eventual release, instead of holding him for the grave.

When you consider that 90 percent of everyone in prison now will be released some day, this attitude implemented now would awaken a real self-interest in these men about their own lives; and such a program could also be used to measure progress and determine when a man could be released. To enforce an authoritarian position upon the imprisoned, with its rigid controls, only benumbs the spirit needed to resolve guilt and increases the intolerance of the future that he inherits anyway. There is just no excuse for making sick people sicker and therefore more of a threat to society when they return to it.

Prison today isn't working in behalf of the individual: the men expend their labor in housekeeping roles and too little of their effort (or none at all) in feeble, face-saving, treatment programs that exist in name only. This isn't enough; such programs to change attitudes are needed to stave off the negative drive of prison that emasculates the future by infecting the man with an insidious "I don't give a damn" rebuttal for not caring. This is how he shuns the indifference of prison, and once joining his host in a symbiotic embrace, he only exists not to care. Nor to love; but potentially, always to hate and destroy what he doesn't understand or what he has escaped from. Yet the great majority of prisoners endure, with a proud, unyielding spirit that will not bend to prison: men who are capable in one moment of an act of tremendous human charity toward another man they hardly know — and in the same instant recipients or purveyors of vicious cruelty.

There is Alvin, my friend with the bucket, who comes and goes during the day to fill up his pail at the faucet near the end of the range. He is undeniably a gentleman, and although his infirmities have left him to stumble and shuffle about, his flair in making the courteous gesture recalls a better day he might have had — not when Alvin was more a gentleman, but when there was less of prison.

At some time during the last seventeen years, not the first seventeen of his thirty-four in prison, Alvin's knees buckled for good, and his walk today resembles the movements of a puppet; he is straight-backed but always bending too much at the knees, as if unsure what the strings are doing. Someone jokingly suggested that Alvin's posture resulted from a parole board hearing, "Afterwards he just buckled and has stayed that way";

but recently someone told me he suffered a stroke a while back which brought about the disability.

Regardless of his "dipsy-doodle" walk, Alvin always manages to arrive where he's going, outfitted in brown prison coat, a white beard that doesn't add any age to his leathery face, and a cap perched to the point of falling off his head.

When he stops to talk with me he sets the bucket down as if it were a stage prop, then launches into the longest sentence he will speak all day: "Why, good morning, Mr. Gentleman!" or, "It's good to see you, sir!" And said warmly, as though we shared, in his smile behind the words, some special secret together for the small courtesies in our relationship. While preparing to answer one of my questions Alvin gazes intently into my face while pursing his lips into a "Huuummm" or "Ooohhh" that is followed by a word or two.

And though he has little himself of life's necessities, I'll find apples on my chair that he "recovers" on his walks I know not where; for he has given up trying to offer me one of his too few cigarettes that are hard to come by after you do this much time in prison, for that outside well has run dry. And yet his laughing voice and generous smile I look for every day.

I always find myself asking the same question, over and over: How many other men, the officials as well, know Alvin that well; for after one is around prison this many years, what else does he have left to give except Alvin?

Whatever my crime was, I never thought of it being criminal; yet my folly was directed against society as well as myself; and I am for upholding the laws although there are no statutes on the law books that cover these kinds of situations. But if a man needs help in the form of something not available to purchase, not even to steal, then he must look upon his incarceration as a new opportunity to search for it within himself. In this

way prison (for me only) became a personal salvation
outside of the usual religious concept meaning to be
"saved." (The Bible-belters are in a large way responsible
for prison being the way it is; they will not have the
opportunity to lay claim to my soul as well.)

If one can accept this explanation of my present
circumstances — that I came to prison with more education
and experiences of life than the average prisoner — then
undoubtedly one can understand my reluctance in asking
anything from prison or anyone imprisoned that I
wouldn't first ask of myself.

There is no need of viewing my life from afar when
the last experience that brought me here was no less
grievous (to me) than the first one which did not; but
during a twelve-year interim I laid the foundation upon
which the commission of this act could be reached:
in a step-by-step rejection of responsibility for self could
a pinnacle of complete irresponsibility be surmounted and
yet, since I foisted on others this indifference towards
self, go unrecognized — until I was forced to accept the
blame.

Many, however, don't come to prison armed with
such ripe circumstances, which later burst on their prison conscience,   nor with my irony of being on the
threshold of capturing this elusive knowledge; I had begun to care for the first time, but too late to save me
from this fate. Fate. . . because there is no guarantee
of ever leaving; one does not know the day or year or
half-century; and within this melting pot of men together, forever strangers, boils a hatred of all things
prison, eternally ready to explode. There are those who
would kill Alvin if prison were theirs to run, for no
other reasons than madness — because Alvin is old and
handicapped, and that is thought to be weakness by
a man who already has made many mistakes in thinking in the course of a warped and terrible history.
But prison has many such abnormal conditions that
cannot be seen by the eye.

For me prison is but a thrust of time between a yet uncertain polarity, between an old life and a potentially new self-awareness that must rest uneasily in my mind until conviction proves it true.

But when will it be time to write of prison? After the animal-like wariness disappears, when memories of human injustice and outraged decency no longer flog the sensibilities with shame? Or will it take a new life of living first to fill up cracks and crevices made in prison, to find a balm for all the lasting loneliness?

And what about the recollections. . . the memories now in present tense — will they then become light and airy wisps of the imagination after one forgets the pain? Or can we check them at the door on leaving, like a coat too bothersome to wear, when our dispositions only want free fresh air? Could these memories come back to haunt us then, from total recall, as the disembodied spirit of our prison past (complete with clanking keys and whisperous soliloquies)?

But now time stands still, a gawking bystander at this fray, who totals all the moments up without bothering to explain what the minutes mean: that Halloween is now, today, yet ushering in All Saints' Day; a day whose birthday it is for a man who is turning thirty; but we are blinded by the insignificance of that day.

Outside the skies are weeping for the dying fall; the last brown leaf flits across a once green lawn, casting mournful glances at that bare-bosomed tree now left naked against the autumn's breeze. And now the rain; I wonder if everywhere it is raining?

And the men huddle together telling jokes and sharing silent sorrows in the cold, talking about the rain, about the prison and the rain. They stand solitary these groups, one apart from another, on corners of streets named South and Industrial Row, afraid of coming rheumatism and hobbling fears. Prison is older to them in ways that I would first have to live through to understand; their prison grows old with paint-peeling slowness, yet any shade of gray would restore her slatternly appearance. But our human prison dies once slowly; this reimprisonment into a grayer ghost only propels our urge to live free once more into a running madness in our minds that wears out life and limb.

The rain is misting now; everyone seems to be standing around waiting for it to end, to begin life once over again.

I have found out life, now that it is separated from the deadly conceits fostered by advertisers who wish upon me toothpaste with "sex appeal"; and I grow weary thinking perhaps the "sane society" is locked up from what only appears to be, but never really is, the good life. Not that I have found it easier to live; on the contrary, the problem is to discover what life really is and what it means to be alive and full of aliveness. And now the rain is falling all around us.

And I remember hearing in childhood that it rains on the just and unjust alike and therefore the rain is only being honest when puddling on sidewalks to show how unevenly the concrete was laid; or lying in depressions on driveways. A man who listens to the rain is privileged with his own symphony; the raindrops falling evenly, except for one maverick droplet over there in the L-shaped recess, where the corners of our building come together, proposing another rhythm by splattering out of tune. But it is only an eavesdrop and ignored because of its different origin, not accepted.

And the rain is fragile, of misty elegance and beauty. . . a gentle falling-down of truth. But I used that phrase once to describe the beauty of a woman's hair, especially when she "took it down" and the hair fell shimmering around her shoulders, the light about her face like a halo. Her busy-working fingers had feminine grace, tucking and patting the blondness into place, every strand somewhere by style; and always smiling as she worked noticing how this pleased me. Afterwards the hair would frame the face, then full and expressive; the hair long and truly blond. Her features showing youth and beauty. Only when I came close enough to smell its clean fragrance did I notice a tangle of brown and gold hidden there; but it was only a sprinkling and with the closeness, it never mattered. Now I think only of the woman.

Tonight, going to dinner, the rain felt cold and sticky on my face like the baloney looked lying on the aluminum tray next to the doughy apple pie and chicken noodle soup. What a funny sound the baloney makes when two pieces are pulled apart, like tarpaper from a roof or the sound of a magic writing board being cleared. I stared suspiciously at the meat, as a child might at a bowl of Rice Krispies before pouring the milk; but the baloney came up smoothly, which ended the meat mystique for one evening.

Apple pie in prison is a Sunday night staple, and when it's properly prepared, something of a treat: light crust with apples cut small and baked until done. Not so tonight though, and it leaves me wondering if we should tolerate such deviations in a dessert "as American as apple pie." I have thought seriously of dropping a note to my congressman about so patriotic a matter, especially since nationalism seems to be at an all-time low! My optimism though is hinged on a cookbook now being prepared for the kitchen, which includes perhaps a recipe for apple pie.

The day has run down into the hours when prison happens to you in a more personal way, without all the necessary and meaningless interruptions around to invade your premises and steal away the time. Lock-up happens about five p.m. during the winter, with the sounds of men working in their cells becoming less and less until the lights go out at ten p.m., and then the face of my plain-Jane prison finally turns into the darkened corners of the cellhouse.

At that hour I move my chair close to the bars to

write by light coming from the officer's desk and to
speculate with the water boy about the price one must
eventually pay to be his own man. A gentle moment of
prison life one never finds in films: one man sitting
outside another's cell, the unspoken part of their conversation the most important since it never really needs
saying.

It is daylight inside my head but growing darker in
this cell that chains my heart to grief, and I can no longer
write about the things of life inside good thoughts; they
at last spin away and spinning faster and faster into
a pirouette-like dream (that whirling could set it free),
fall to tiredness in a bow settling deeper inside me,
to become lost by spreading a drowsy warmth around
and around me. But now the rain is gone; I can no
longer see through darkness at the falling, nor hear
the rain sounds on the roof, but sounds inside my cell
remain. Only one thought remains: I am the range-
tender for these thirty-three men (tending the lost sheep?),
but who tends me? For I am lost, as lost as these thirty-
three. I am lashed by waves of desolation on this empty
journey, hearing louder sounds than that sea of voices
in the mess hall; I cry out for a sea of faith not to let
me drown all alone—into this murky shell of life. For
a prisoner I will always be, always the imprisoned self
in this lifetime.

And now that shadowy prison range outside my prison
door becomes life's highway, and walking slowly towards
me in the darkness of my vision come Alvin and the
water boy and a painter I once knew and another
prison friend, a poet; they are calling out to me but I
am locked in and then I know why my vision is so
poor because sleep is falling faster into my eyes than I
can stop, mistress of my senses no one sees, yet whispering softly as she reaches out her hand, "There is still
another day coming."

Bittersweet: A Recollection
by William R. Baker

I heard the bell ring in the hallway outside of the classroom, and all of us children, laughing, pushing and shoving, spilled out into the hallway. Suddenly, above the chatter, some of the boys and girls began to chant: "School's out, school's out; the teacher's let the fools out!"

Like the rest of the kids, I dashed outside, into the rain that had begun to fall earlier on that September day. I was also happy; I laughed and played with the rest of the kids. It was Friday, and now I would have all weekend to spend at home with Big Mama who was sick in bed.

Every day after school I would run the five blocks from the school to my house on Saint Clara Street, anticipating the moment I would once again be around the people I knew and loved. It had only been three weeks now since I was first taken to School No. 4 to begin my schooling, and I had not yet gotten used to being away from home. I also rushed home every day because I enjoyed the fuss Big Mama made over me when I got right up in the big four-posted brass bed with her and told her about my day in school, or when I got her a glass of water and listened to her telling me about how she would soon be leaving me cause she had to go home to sweet Jesus and how she wanted me to be the little man of the house.

By the time I had gone two blocks from school I

was drenched. The rain was falling like a million showers had been turned on in the sky and someone had
forgotten to turn them off. I reached the Avenue and,
after looking both ways, I dashed across and turned
into the alley that ran alongside my house.

I hadn't got far up the alley before I knew something was wrong. I could see my house and parked
in front of it were three or four cars that didn't belong
there. Putting on a burst of speed I cut across a couple
of yards and headed for my back door 'cause it was
the closest. It must have taken me a minute to realize
that the door was locked. I broke around to the front.
Two men were coming out of the front door carrying
a long, funny-looking basket. I pushed past the two
men, entered the house, and made for Big Mama's
room.

At first the room looked empty because Big Mama's
brass bed was gone. I saw four new-looking spots on
the rug where the bed had stood. Looking around I
saw that someone had undone the bed and leaned
it, the mattress, and the bedsprings against Big Mama's
red-flowered wallpaper. Then I noticed that my dog,
Teddy, was sitting right in the spot where he used
to lay under the foot of Big Mama's bed. Teddy was
howling and howling as if he too knew that Big Mama
was sure to raise cain when she saw how her room was
being messed up. Not knowing what to think, I turned
and walked down the hallway leading to the living
room, from which came the sound of crying, and someone saying over and over: "Big Mama's gone, Big
Mama's gone. Lord Jesus, why did you have to take
her from me." This made me think of Big Mama telling me that she would soon have to be leaving me
to go home to sweet Jesus.

Just as I started into the living room, Mr. Bob, who
lived next door, came out in the hallway and seeing
me he stopped. Big fat tears were running down his
face. I must have stared at him because it was the

first time that I had ever seen a grown man cry. Big Mama was always telling me that I was her little man and that men didn't cry. Mr. Bob dropped to his knees and threw his arms around me and said: "You must be brave, li'l Billy, and don't worry too much." I wasn't worrying then, but I was about to. Looking over Mr. Bob's shoulder I saw the rest of my family seated in the living room and all of them were crying. I still didn't understand what was going on but when I saw Little Mama, my mother, crying, I started bawling myself. Mr. Bob was hugging me harder and harder. Between sobs, I asked him: "Where is Big Mama?" I had to repeat it two or three times before he said, "Big Mama's gone to meet sweet Jesus." I already knew this from hearing everybody, including Big Mama herself, saying it. I said, "Yessir, I know that, but where is she meeting him?" With that he turned his head away and stammered: "Down to. . . uh. . . um. . . Mr. Allen's."

I twisted out of his arms, ran out of the house, and sped down the alley toward the avenue and Mr. Allen's. I knew where Mr. Allen's place was because Marie, my older sister, had taken me there one day. I remembered the flowers and the people crying and wailing, and Mr. Allen standing up passing out handkerchiefs and saying to the people: "Don't worry, Jesus will take care of everything." I didn't know what I was going to say to this Jesus when I saw him down to Mr. Allen's, but I wasn't about to let him take Big Mama anyplace.

With my lungs almost bursting I finally reached the rear of Mr. Allen's place. When I entered the back door I didn't see anyone. I stood in a little room with a long table in it. The shelves around the walls were filled with bottles and long tubes and big jars. The whole place smelled funny. I walked on through the room and through three more until I came to the front room of the building where I saw a big man standing by a telephone.

He looked at me and said, "What are you doing

messing around here, boy?" I told him that I had come to see my Big Mama who was here to meet Jesus. He looked at me real funny and said, "What's your Mama's name, son?"

"Betty Wright."

"Oh, just one moment."

He picked up the telephone and called a number and whispered something to somebody. The next thing I knew my whole family was swarming through the door. They took me home, telling me that I would get to see Big Mama before she left.

Two days later my mother made me take a bath and put on my Sunday clothes, and along with the rest of the family I walked down to Mr. Allen's. There were all kinds of cars parked in front of Mr. Allen's and I saw lots of people that I usually saw only on Thanksgiving and Christmas: cousins, aunts, uncles, and a lot of old women from Big Mama's church. They were all lined up, passing by a real pretty, long pink box. All around the box were flowers, red and white and yellow. When I reached the front of the box, Mr. Bob picked me up to look in it, and I saw Big Mama. She had on her favorite blue dress and her string of pearls. Around me I heard people whispering: "Don't she look natural." "Just like she's asleep." I called to Big Mama: "Big Mama, why do you want to go home with sweet Jesus? Don't you know that your home is here with me and that I would never leave you to go with anybody?"

After I had spoken it seemed that everyone began to cry and wail louder. Then Mr. Allen started moving through the crowd passing out white napkins and saying that Big Mama had done her work here on earth and now must go home to rest with Jesus.

The next morning, before anybody else had wakened, I crawled out of bed and wandered into Big Mama's room. Teddy, my dog, was still lying in the same spot. I walked over and sat down beside him.

Rehabilitation and Treatment
by Joe Martinez

The convict strolled into the prison administration building to get assistance and counseling for his personal problems. Just inside the main door were several other doors, proclaiming: *Parole, Counselor, Chaplain, Doctor, Teacher, Correction,* and *Therapist.*

The convict chose the door marked *Correction,* inside of which were two other doors: *Custody* and *Treatment.* He chose *Treatment,* and was confronted with two more doors, *Juvenile* and *Adult.* He chose the proper door and again was faced with two doors: *Previous Offender* and *First Offender.* Once more he walked through the proper door, and, again, two doors: *Democrat* and *Republican.* He was a Democrat; and so he hurried through the appropriate door and ran smack into two more doors; *Black* and *White.* He was black; and so he walked through that door — and fell nine stories to the street.

Untitled
by George Page

Lincoln Elementary School had once been a white school, but the whites had abandoned it long ago and left it for us. It was only a short walk from the Union Station, which stood at the threshold of the giant structures of one of the great commercial centers of the world: "Downtown St. Louis." Our house was two blocks from the school, a two-storied brick building turned dull and dirty by the smoke and soot of the city. It seemed like the teachers never had the time to show us anything, nor did they seem to have a great amount of interest. I remember my arithmetic teacher, Mr. Mosley. I asked him to help me after class with some problems and he told me that he did not have the time but for me not to worry because he would pass me anyway. Of course, I never learned. And after that I hardly did any work in his class. Grade school was not too eventful and I graduated easily enough.

I remember our house well. We had two rooms and a kitchen; the kitchen, however, was shared with three other families so we had to take turns in using it. There were no specific times for anyone to use it, and that caused many of the arguments between the tenants which erupted in the building. I remember the roaches in our kitchen. They were an institution. At no hour during the day or night could anyone enter our kitchen and not be greeted by our host, the roach. But we learned to accept and live with them. We had learned "co-existence," because no amount of cleaning or DDT would even faze them.

The rats were not as numerous, nor as brave. They would only come out of their holes at night. But it was an established fact that St. Louis really belonged to the rats, or at least it seemed so in the section that I am from. They were like burglars; their methods of entry to any cupboard or bureau drawer were amazing. It became a battle of wits between my mother and the rats.

Since there were no playgrounds in our neighborhood, we naturally played in the streets. We played football and baseball. I remember how angry us kids used to get if someone would park their car on one of our bases, and when this happened we would simply use the car for a base. It is difficult to slide into third when the base is someone's front fender.

We lived one block from Market Street, which is one of the widest and busiest streets in the city. It was a main artery from downtown to the suburbs, and during the morning and evening rush hours it was impossible to cross on foot, or even by car. I will never know how many lives Market Street has claimed. I know that when I was eight years old I saw my buddy, Lester Bosman, killed there by a nice white man who dragged him for two blocks under his front bumper.

I carried the habit of not studying from grade school to high school, and for the first two years at Sumner High I skated by on the skin of my teeth. But after I reached my third year, I found that I had to study for certain tests and the final examinations. I never cut too many classes, only the study periods; however, my parents had to come to the school at least twice a year.

Sumner High School was originally built for about

three thousand students, but at the time I went there the students exceeded nine thousand. I had at first planned to attend Washington Tech which was downtown and closer to where I lived, but my father, who had just returned from the navy, forced me to go to Sumner, which was on the west side of town and quite a distance from my house. Sumner was said to have a higher academic standard than Washington Tech, but I was scared to go there because of one of the most feared gangs in St. Louis, the "Termites." I knew that I would be in for it. I was a member of the "Counts," a downtown gang, but most of the gang, being older than me, had already dropped out of school. I couldn't tell all this to my father who had quit his packinghouse job to become, of all things, a policeman. And so I had to enroll at Sumner.

The first couple of days I could not avoid the bigger and tougher guys and I was given several beatings. When I went to see the Assistant Principal he told me that he was sorry but that there was nothing he could do. That evening I went home determined to put a stop to these beatings. It was easy for me to steal my father's service revolver because he worked at night and slept in the day. And the next day when I went to school, the secretary of the Termites slapped me and I shot him. But the bullet only nicked his ear. After that I fired two more times down the hallway of the school. Since the students were changing classes and there were hundreds in the hallway, it is a miracle that nobody was hit. Of course I was suspended after that, but only for a week. When I returned to school things were different; I never had any more trouble.

I started drinking wine during my junior year. I was already smoking pot; it was also somewhat of an institution; all of the older guys did it. I would hang around with them and they would give me the "roaches." I was about fourteen then and had not learned how to inhale so I never really got high in those days. Later, though, after a little practice, I got my first real reefer high. It was like being born again, like the religious converts who have "seen the light." During my study period I would sneak out of school and get high off pot and wine, then return to my English class. The teacher knew that I was high but she never said anything. The students had a habit of beating up teachers — especially women teachers.

In due course I graduated from high school, and because I had turned out to be a pretty good basketball player I had a chance to go to college. I had decided to go to Winston-Salem, North Carolina, and maybe I would've if I hadn't got busted.

Ever since I was about fifteen I had been tight with a guy called House Mouse. He had quit school some time before and was just hanging around on the corner. His brother dealt reefers around the neighborhood, and every night House Mouse and I would go to his brother's apartment and roll up his joints and put them in a match box for him. Then his brother would give us a half-dollar each and turn us on with some reefers. I don't remember how long this went on, but one day the cops busted in and all of us were arrested. House Mouse and I were taken to the Juvenile Center of the House of Correction. House Mouse got two years because he already had a police record. When I was taken before the judge he gave me an ultimatum: either I go to the army or serve two years like House Mouse. Naturally, I chose the army. I had to put my age up to enlist.

In the army I experienced my first real personal encounter with whites; it was in 1951 and the army had been "integrated." In my neighborhood I had had very little dealings with whites, only the insurance man, gas and light man, and the like. But none of my own age. At first impression the white guys in the army seemed

like anybody else to me. I made some very close friends
all the way through ("some of my best friends are
white"). After basic training I was shipped to Greenland. I was a radar operator and a mechanic on B-17s
in the Air Rescue. I was the only black man in my
crew, but I never tried to "set an example" or "prove
myself." Then I began to listen to "Moscow Molly" over
Radio Moscow every evening at six o'clock. And for
the first time in my life I saw the white man in a different light. I was aware of the white problem in America but in a very limited sense, having never taken the
time to look into it very thoroughly. It was then, in
Greenland, in 1952, that I first became consciously
outraged and confused. The confusion has since disappeared but not the anger. It has become more refined and reenforced throughout the years.

The confusion, however, was still with me when I
was discharged from the army and returned home
to St. Louis, to the same rats, the same roaches, and
the same slums patrolled by the same white policemen and the few black-white policemen. I looked long
and hard at the terrible poverty, at the seemingly hap-
less plight of my people and their apathy towards it.
And in my confusion and fear and sorrow I dived
into the dope-world head first. The years of fighting
my fear of the white man and the confusion of trying
to live in the world of his creation are inexpressible.

Now the confusion is gone — not only for myself,
but for thousands like me. I will no longer accept a
system which governs by sucking the blood of colored
people.

An Old-Timer
Looks at 42 Years Behind Walls
by R. L. Moseley

[Actually R. L. "Whitey" Moseley has been in prison
for forty-three years. For the past year he has been
a "trusty" outside the walls. Whitey is one of the most
respected of the old-timers. He is a well-kept, self-pos-
sessed man of sixty-three, with steely gray hair and
a clear gaze. I don't know what crime he was convicted
of. One does not ask Whitey Moseley such questions.
— *E. K.*]

The prison crouched between barren sand dunes in
a remote and lonely corner of the state, a sprawling
collection of unfeeling stone and grim, cold steel. The
year was 1924, and I was twenty years old. Many men
already knew it as twenty-three acres of venomous
hate, surrounded by towering gray walls. As the grisly
abode of 1,800 living dead, it seethed with raw, ele-
mental passions spawned of colorless days and endless
nights spent in a graveyard of human hope.

When the massive steel gates rolled open and a man
was admitted to serve his time, his head was shorn
of all hair; he was dressed in a coarse gray uniform
and imprisoned in a tiny, almost bare cell. A deathly
silence ruled the gloomy corridors of the prison in
those days— broken only at given times by the racket

of slamming cell doors in a cadence that plainly echoed
the resentment stored in embittered hearts. One could
feel the crushing weight of prison rule, the total suppression, as the iron jaws of the massive cellblocks
worked at their ceaseless grinding on human souls.
One strained his ears to catch a human sound, but
there was none. All was still as the final grave. The
spirit of the stoutest man felt annihilated.

The Silent System in effect then reduced everybody
to using signs whenever communication was necessary.
It was a piece of wry humor to raise the hand, receive
a nod from the glum guard on his little raised dais
in the shops, approach him and motion that one had
to "go." A wooden paddle hung on a nail at his desk.
The "goer" took the paddle and walked with it in hand
to a two-closet affair shielded only by a halfway par-
tition and hung the wooden paddle on the outside of
the halfway door. The time that the paddle was returned
to the desk indicated how long the "goer" had been
absent from his task of work. [A task is a prescribed
amount of work. *E. K.*] There was no chance for stalling,
or goldbricking, for the paddle "snitched" by its very
whereabouts.

The shops, under contract labor, contained many
iron-wrought spittoons, for smoking in the shops was
not allowed, and cigarettes were unheard of. Prisoners
chewed tobacco while at work, and used the spittoons
on occasion to clobber some enemy when arguments
or differences cropped up. Tension was always at a
high peak, as each man literally slaved over his task.
Despite the Silent System, men did manage to communi-
cate, for on Saturdays, in season, tier by tier of men
marched to the drill ground to watch a baseball game.
Under the broiling sun they sat bunched together on
wooden benches, unable to smoke because smoking was
forbidden anyplace save three times a night in the cells.
A kind of cellblock trusty passed a light from cell to

cell, carrying a flaming torch like the eternal flame used at the Olympics.

Mail and a weekly newspaper were excessively censored, with items cut out or obliterated by the censors. It was a violation of rules to have a pencil, ink, paper, or anything in the tiny cells, excepting a towel, two library books, comb, and a piece of soap. The walls were barren of pictures — a *rocking* chair, a toilet bowl, and a wash basin were the only fixtures. Attendance at ball games, two-reel movies, and chapel was compulsory.

Everybody worked. The aged mended prisoners' sox, the lame led the blind around the grounds, picking up bits of stray paper and leaves. There was, it seemed, a heartless efficiency about routines, day after endless day, year upon colorless year. There being so little for diversion, the average inmate deteriorated, suffering from mental inertia, frustrated and oppressed by the futility of his daily existence.

The hundreds of ways in which the spirit of man was affected for no good by the negation, suppression, and total regimentation in those early years gradually disappeared, or altered their impact with the passage of time. About 1933 the federal government passed a law forbidding the shipment of prison-made goods out of the state; and that helped to abolish contract labor, and at the same time idled hundreds of men. Adjustments came. The Silent System was broken. Men began to look alive as they called or talked or whistled or sang as they pleased, except in the main dining room. It was 1942 before talking at meals was allowed. Many of the oppressive, petty and irksome rules were dropped — the prison took on an atmosphere of controlled but less rigorous living. Ah, it was still prison, but without the narrowness. By the simple expedient of the turning of official eyes, inmates were allowed to make their cells more livable: put up a few family pictures, secure a table, have pencils, pens, ink, paints, drafting equipment and hobby crafts.

Time has changed many things, but prison is still prison. It still crouches between barren sand dunes and the walls still hem in the men, killing their souls and crushing their spirits.

Old-Timer,
Inside 42 Years, Sees Outside
by R. L. Moseley

The first day was a blur. Impressions crowded my mind like a movie screen gone haywire: cars whizzed by, people in street clothes, tall trees, the bright blue free air. All I distinctly remember is that I was nervous and sweating as the officer of the outside dormitory assigned my bunk, and that I spent the remainder of the afternoon at a window in the dormitory, looking down the highway. It was strange, and nice, to be able to see a distance without having my vision broken by walls. I slept well the first night, probably because of nervous exhaustion.

The next morning I reported for work. The boss said, "Whitey, you go with the potato detail today." So I jumped into this snazzy auto and was driven to Zorn's, located downtown. Zorn's is an old brewery, solid as a jail in construction. On the way I saw many homes reminiscent of free days long ago. Hundreds of autos of all shades and colors. Not much traffic, although Michigan City impressed me as a thriving community for its size. Saw one gal on the sidewalks. Weather was cold on this date, only a few people at large. Watched a guy tote a bale of hay to his car and dump it in on the nice upholstery. Passed several churches and a couple schools where the kids' bicycles were parked neatly in rows in the schoolyard.

73

Later in the day I took a leisurely ride about the limits of the state grounds. Stopped by the prison's cemetery, where about two hundred rest in separate graves, beneath identifying headstones. Did *not* select a lot at this time. Also visited the nearby greenhouse where flowers for the prison are grown. Imagine!

The next outing was to the prison's dairy farm — Summitt Farm, officially. It is located about nine miles from the prison and the ride was eye-filling. Zooming along the highway, past woods and lots, homes and farms, with here and there an auto sales yard floundering in all kinds of bargains for the early bird. Saw a freight train loaded with military equipment for Vietnam. Passed several motels, neon-lighted. The air was bracing, the sky somewhat overcast, but nothing could dampen my interest in the passing scene after forty-two years of bars and steel!

                    *   *   *

The grounds outside the walls are twice the size of the prison compound. I am assigned to what is called "general custody detail" — which means that you do any and everything. There are a few permanent assignments, but most of the guys out here have made parole and are waiting to go home. And while they wait, they work.

A coal pile as big as a mountain stares the initiate in the face, and with a smile he is handed a nice, big scoop shovel. Get with it, man, get with it! Muscles ache, bones creak, but that coal has got to go. Without it, the prison would have no heat, no lights, and no hot water. Dishes would remain dirty, laundry would go unwashed. Mighty important, yeah man!

There are lawns to mow, trees to plant, flowers to raise, grounds to clear of debris. Trucks fly to and fro, each with a load of sand or dirt or slop and innumerable errands all requiring a conveyance of one sort or another. There are birdhouses to build, squirrels to feed, officers' families to service.

Is it raining? Snowing? Blowing? Pay it no mind, duty calls and, buddy, you'd better get with it. But actually, it's not as harsh a detail as all that. Time passes quickly with something to do. There are plenty of showers in the dormitory and a cot to flop on when you're beat out. After the day's work, there's television to watch, games to play and reading material to suit every taste. Mail call is important; some guys have been waiting a long time for a letter with the offer or guarantee of a job so that they can go home. It's a terrible mental strain to have made parole and then to be held here for lack of a job.

General custody detail operates under the direction of an outside captain, an outside deputy warden, and two regular officers. The idea of working at such a terrific pace, it is said, is to get the parolee in shape for any job he goes to when he is released. The pay is twenty cents per day, seven days a week. One half of this sum is held back until a man accumulates $35 — which is *going home* money.

*   *   *

I was both pleased and saddened when the past month's clemency returns arrived a few days ago. In the first instance, a long-timer finally made the grade. He received a commutation of his life term after serving over thirty years. On the other hand, another lifer with over thirty-six years served was denied a commutation. One wonders what yardstick is used to determine a yea or a nay. Like the Little Fooler in the *Chicago Tribune*, you have to work hard at that one.

The plan to allow selected men to work outside and return to prison at night is gaining momentum in penal circles. I assume that by "selected" is meant those men who have paroles but who cannot secure employment.

In any case, working for wages would be a boon and a boost to morale. The average person leaving prison today, unless he has other means, seldom has enough money to get himself a decent start. Men with families will be able to provide for them and also to save a little for themselves if this progressive step jells. I hope it does.

One time in *Reader's Digest* there was an article, written by a businessman, entitled, "Keep Your Convicts." The businessman claimed that inmates are trained on outmoded machines while imprisoned and are unable to operate modern machines when released. There is a great deal of truth in what he says, but what I see is the businessman's attitude toward prisoners who, by force, have to learn on the machines provided in the prisons of the land. In brief, the businessman would not want men released from servitude simply because he feels that they could not function in society. One wonders if he would make an investment in a potential labor pool and donate some modern machines to prison vocational shops?

If and when men reach the moon and it seems possible to establish communities thereon, look for the "drafting" of long-term prisoners. They will be "exiled" to the moon, to build roads, dig ditches, and prepare the land for the erection of buildings and homes. It will be cheap labor, easily commanded. I recall that when England settled Australia, prisoners were sent to that raw land for the very purpose cited. Exile. The oldest form of man's punishment for man. Ask Adam.

The Trip

by Clarence Harris

CAST

Tip . . . . Negro with natural hairstyle and a beard. Middle twenties.

Satin . . . . Negro with processed hairstyle and conservative dress. Middle twenties.

Gino . . . . White. Hippie style. Middle twenties.

Carl . . . . Negro. Middle thirties. Well dressed.

Landlady . . . . . Negro. Middle age. Bandannaed head.

First Cop . . . . . White. Uniformed.

Second Cop. . . . White. Uniformed.

Lt. Clanahan . . . White. Plainclothes.

Coroner . . . . . . White. Suit.

PROPS

Music: African bata drum, bongos, brass, bass.

Animal smells; animal noises: growls, roars.

Two bed sheets, a chair, a table with phone, an African spear and shield, a knife, two blank pistols.

NIGHT STREET SCENE

Tip dashes onstage from right. Satin saunters on from left. Music: Up-tempo, drums, bongos. Tip collides with Satin.

SATIN: Hey! Watch where you going! He-ey! What's happening, Tip?

TIP: You seen Gino, Satin? I've got to find him in a hurry, man. [*With urgency*]. . . Got to git back!

SATIN: Back where?

TIP: Gotta finish my trip. . . .they waiting on me. . . . Yeah. . . .they waiting. . . .have you seen him? . . . . where is he?

SATIN: Who. . .Gino? Aw. . .yeah...but wait a minute man. . .tell me who you got waiting on you—some skin I know? What is it? A party?

TIP: Naw. . .You wouldn't dig what I mean.

SATIN: What you mean? I ain't no lame, you know! Say! how's about turning me on? [*Enthusiastic.*] Like I'll pay you back as soon as my woman bring my bread in tonight. You know I will too.

TIP: Fuck that shit!—tell me where I can find Gino. I'm in a hurry. . .done wasted too much time already. . . goofing with you. Where is he, dammit! [*Shouts.*] Tell me! Tell me!

SATIN: Look. . .'bout that turn-on, now. . .

TIP: Tell me. . .tell me. . .ya fool. . .where is he? Where is he? [*Screaming and shaking Satin.*] I gotta get back. . .they won't wait too long. . .gotta get back...

SATIN: Cool it, man. . .cool it. . .say, baby! don't get so frantic with my threads, ya hear? Are ya gonna turn me on?

TIP: You can't go where I'm going. . .you ain't no king. . .you ain't even living. . .ha! ha!. . .Continentaled down. . .hair slicked. . .yeah. . .just look at ya! Who're you, man. . .where you come from, looking like a white man's clown!

SATIN: You know me, baby. . .I am Satin. . .I am your ace man. You must have bailed out—else you just been crazy all the time. Must be spacing to talk to me like that. . . Yeah, I seen Gino standing outside the Bird's Nest. . .Say. . .wait a minute. . .all right!. . .

[*shouting to the departing Tip*]. . .then later for you, you dingbat. . .hope the man busts you, running 'round all frantic. . .grabbing people. . .bet you kill your damn self. [*Walks off right.*]

[*Gino and Carl walking on, left.*]

GINO: Man! Ain't life beautiful!

CARL: Beautiful. . . beau. . .ti. . .ful, baby!

GINO: Love is the thing — hey, Carl?

CARL: [*Dancing around.*] Love!. . .love. . .I love... luv-luv-luv!

GINO: Say, look who's coming — well! if it ain't old Tip, the black boy that don't dig us whiteys. What you want — some sugar, Tip? Ha ha ha [*nudges Carl*]. Yeah, sweet whitey Gino — that's me! Ha ha ha.

TIP: Can that crap, Gino, and give me 2,000 mgs of acid — quick!

GINO: You gotta catch a train, Tip? Going on a trip, huh? Ha ha. Who's waiting on you? One of those blond, blue-eyed devil broads you hate so much? [*Nudges Carl, who bends, holding his stomach and laughing.*] Dig this lame, Carl, ain't he a gas?

TIP: [*Pulls a knife, menacing.*] You faggot, give me that jive 'fo I cut your fucking throat. [*Lunges but misses.*]

GINO: [*Jumping behind Carl.*] All right, all right! Like, man. . .a joke's a joke. . .no rough stuff. . .okay? Okay, Tip? — Cool. Give it to him, Carl. [*Tip pockets knife, cops stuff, and walks offstage, left.*]

GINO: [*Keeping eye on Tip.*] Say, baby, what's happening with that cat? You see that — did you dig that!

CARL: Yeah. . .real weird, a weirdo. . .uh, huh, a real weirdo!

GINO: Cats like that now. . .cause you spades to blow your connect. . .like we got to stick together, you know?. . .like, love, man. . .that's where it's at. . .I like colored guys. . .ain't I always treated you right, Carl? Don't I look out fer you?

SCENE II

Door prop. Landlady singing spiritual and sweeping. Tip enters, right. Music: slow.

LANDLADY: I want to see you.

TIP: Out of my way, old woman.

LANDLADY: Humph! Old woman, huh? Well you needs to learn respeck for old folks, and anyhow, I wants that back rent you owes. Mr. Stein says I can't let nobody git behind agin. . .I gotta git that rent— he ain't gonna stand for no stuff, either!

TIP: Dammit, woman—move! I ain't got time to listen to your ravings and preachings. . .I'm in a hurry and I ain't gonna ast you no more. . .

LANDLADY: Now listen here—don't you go gitting uppity wit me, boy. I am a Christian woman and ain't gon' take no cussing from the likes sich as you.

TIP: If I don't respect you, what you gonna do, you old Aunt Jemima, what you gonna do? [*Pushes past her. She draws back broom at him.*]

LANDLADY: I'm gonna whup your head with this broom, that's what I gon' do! Boy is you crazy. . . Naw. . .you on that dope! That's what it is. Standing there with your eyes bugging out your head. Lord, Lord, don't know what this world coming to. . .talking 'bout you ain't got time—ain't got time to pay your rent, that's for sho. . .got time to play them crazy records. . .beat on them drums. . .try to jump on poor decent folks like me. . .must think you better'n other folks. . .[*grows angrier*] well, you just git. . .git outta here—go on! [*Backing away from door and holding broom threateningly.*]

TIP: You old Uncle Tom, stop jeffing so much. Mr. Stein! Ha ha. People like you what keeps us from being men. . .decent! Ha ha. Old man Stein's son is the one sells dope that you hate so much. Oh, yeah! to us black folks. Look at you—look like you on a plantation. . .

Where's your cotton sack, woman? [*Laughs. Opens door.*] Go collect the rent from the roaches and rats. Kings like me don't pay no rent—yes, I am a king— King Oobee-doobee-dee, that's me. . . ha ha ha.

LANDLADY: I bet you git out when I come back with the poleece. Just wait and see. I'm gonna git 'em.... ain't gon' have no dope fiends jumping on me, not while the Lord's willing! [*Walks off, right.*]

TIP: [*shouting into the room*] It's me; I'm back; here I am. . .over here. . .you still here?

Music: slow, bongos. . .batas!

TIP: Is it time to dance?

Lights out. Music: tempo-up. Animal growls, roars, smells. All inside room.

SCENE III

Lights on. Landlady enters, right, with two uniformed policemen.

LANDLADY: [*pointing to door of room*] This hit theah, officers.

FIRST COP: Stand over there, gal, we'll see how bad he is! [*Knocks.*] It's the police! Police. . .open up, boy! We know you're in there.

SECOND COP: By God, boy—open up, you hear me? Nigger, if we have to break in and get you, you'll wish you never was born.

FIRST COP: This's one of them mean coons, Bill. . . You kick in the door and I'll cover you. . .ready? Let's go!

Crash. Lights out. Drums, animal roars, human screams, pistol shots. Drums— faster, then suddenly stop.

SCENE IV

Lights on. Landlady sitting in chair, sobbing. Coroner looking under sheet at body. Plainclothes policeman downstage at phone.

LT. CLANAHAN: Hello—chief? Yeah, Clanahan. . . looks like we might wrap this up soon as we find the killer. . . what? uh huh. . .two cops. . .yeah, I know. . . that's five policemen lost this year. Yeah, chief, we're doing the best we can. Witnesses? Well, we got five tenants who heard a crash and the shots. . .one eyewitness right here—the landlady. She saw it all, she's the one called the cops. . .she's hysterical now—in a shock or something. . .keeps babbling something about a Zulu with a spear and shield and—get this, chief—lions and tigers. . .what? yeah, soon as I get the doc's report. . . . If we could only find the killer. . .he took the knife with him. I put out an all-points bulletin with a description of the suspect. Okay, chief. . .see you downtown! [*Lt. Clanahan walks over and pats landlady on shoulder encouragingly.*] Now! now! don't take it so hard. . . try to relax now. . .pull yourself together.

LANDLADY: Lord, Lord, have mercy. [*Voice rising hysterically*] I seen it, I seen it. . .I did. . .

LT. CLANAHAN: Now, now. . .

LANDLADY: He was standing right there with that long spear. . .it was terrible. . .Lord. . .them big cats— lions. . .and they was clawing and clawing. . .growling . . . . Then the Lord pertecked me, cause I fainted.

LT. CLANAHAN: Hmmmm! I think you need to lie down and rest. Maybe when you're better we can talk some more. Right now you're upset.

LANDLADY: [*Jumps up, throws arms in air and shouts.*] But they wuz—I tell you! I seen them. . .lions . . .tigers. . .and him standing right there! I seen it.

LT. CLANAHAN: Calm yourself now, and I'll have doc give you something so you can rest. You'll be all right now. They won't be back. Just sit down and relax. [*Landlady sits.*] That's it. . . that's fine. [*Turns to coroner.*] Hey, doc, come here. What did you find out?

CORONER: [*Rises slowly from corpse and walks center, looking back over his shoulder.*] Well, the policemen were stabbed. Twice, at close range, in the chest.

LT. CLANAHAN: Hell, I already know that, but how long did they live? The killer must have hid that knife someplace. . . .

CORONER: [*His eyes still drawn to the corpse.*] Knife? What knife? Who said anything about a knife?

LT. CLANAHAN: I did. . .I mean, you did! You just said that they were stabbed!

CORONER: Damn right. By something about three inches wide with a sharp point and prongs on the rear. . .like, say — a spear.

LT. CLANAHAN: A spear? Doc! are you crazy, too?

CORONER: That ain't all: those policemen have been scarred by cats, big cats. [*He points toward corpse.*] In fact, after finding some tufts of hair over there, I recommend that you check for some tigers and lions on the loose!!

Lights out quickly. Music: drums throbbing. Animal sounds, smells, muted brass. Then lights on. Stage clear except for Tip dressed like Zulu with spear and shield. He dances to music with lights blinking on and off and collapses at curtain.

by
Etheridge
Knight

The Idea of Ancestry

1

Taped to the wall of my cell are 47 pictures: 47 black
faces: my father, mother, grandmothers (1 dead), grand
fathers (both dead), brothers, sisters, uncles, aunts,
cousins (1st & 2nd), nieces, and nephews. They stare
across the space at me sprawling on my bunk. I know
their dark eyes, they know mine. I know their style,
they know mine. I am all of them, they are all of me;
they are farmers, I am a thief, I am me, they are thee.

I have at one time or another been in love with my mother,
1 grandmother, 2 sisters, 2 aunts (1 went to the asylum),
and 5 cousins. I am now in love with a 7 yr old niece
(she sends me letters written in large block print, and
her picture is the only one that smiles at me).

I have the same name as 1 grandfather, 3 cousins, 3 nephews,
and 1 uncle. The uncle disappeared when he was 15, just took
off and caught a freight (they say). He's discussed each year
when the family has a reunion, he causes uneasiness in
the clan, he is an empty space. My father's mother, who is 93
and who keeps the Family Bible with everybody's birth dates
(and death dates) in it, always mentions him. There is no
place in her Bible for "whereabouts unknown."

Each Fall the graves of my grandfathers call me, the brown
hills and red gullies of mississippi send out their electric
messages, galvanizing my genes. Last yr/like a salmon quitting
the cold ocean — leaping and bucking up his birthstream/I
hitchhiked my way from L. A. with 16 caps in my pocket and a
monkey on my back, and I almost kicked it with the kinfolks.
I walked barefooted in my grandmother's backyard/I smelled
   the old
land and the woods/I sipped cornwhiskey from fruit jars with the
   men/
I flirted with the women/I had a ball till the caps ran out
and my habit came down. That night I looked at my grand
   mother
and split/my guts were screaming for junk/but I was almost
contented/I had almost caught up with me.
(The next day in Memphis I cracked a croaker's crib for a fix.)

This yr there is a gray stone wall damming my stream, and
   when
the falling leaves stir my genes, I pace my cell or flop on my
   bunk
and stare at 47 black faces across the space. I am all of them,
they are all of me, I am me, they are thee, and I have no sons
to float in the space between.

The Poor Pay More,
Even for Their Dreams

One of the most familiar replies heard in a black community to the casual greetings, "What'cha know?" and "How're you doing?" is the reply: "Just the same old three-six-nine." The despair and futility, even to the uninitiated, is clearly conveyed in the replier's tone, but to those devotees of the "numbers game" and "dream books," there is still a deeper meaning that sums up in one word, in one symbol, the total attitude of the replier. To such a person, 3-6-9 means shit. According to the "dream books," whenever one dreams of shit he should, immediately upon arising, "play" 3-6-9 with his favorite "numbers writer" — even if it means using the rent money to do so.

In the "numbers game," a player determines (via dream books, license numbers, astrology, hunches, etc.) which numbers he wants to play, and, along with his wager, he gives them to a writer, who usually has a route of steady customers and who usually has established a timetable to be in certain bars, poolrooms, and hangouts. The given numbers, the player's wager and the writer's "mark" are written down, in triplicate, on a small pad called the "slip." The player is given a "slip," the writer keeps one, and the third copy, along with the player's wager, is turned in to a "station."

The winning numbers are determined either by certain digits taken from the *advance, decline,* and *unchanged* columns of the New York Stock Exchange report, or by a "wheel" which is generally a barrel-like device in which, say, a thousand chits, numbered from one to a hundred, are placed. The "wheel" is spun; a given amount of chits are withdrawn from it, and their numbers are recorded on a slip of paper, from which hundreds of mimeographed copies are made and distributed to various "drops" and "stations" throughout the city. Thus, a player, according to the particular organization, can find out if he has "hit" the numbers simply by reading a daily paper, or else by stopping by a "station" and picking up a "drawing."

If a player has chosen the right combination of digits, he wins about $300 for a ten-cent wager. He can also win a lesser amount if three of his four digits have appeared in a predicted sequence. The odds, however, against picking the winning combination from the New York Stock Exchange report is something like one in 15,000. The odds against picking the winning combination from a "policy wheel" is sometimes more, sometimes less; it is left entirely up to the individual "banker" to decide how many chits are to be placed in the "wheel." (Some bankers, in order to establish an honest reputation, sometimes allow a few writers and players to witness a drawing of the chits. And they also contrive "hits" to stimulate business, to make the poor shell out more money for their dreams.)

The numbers operation is highly organized. At the base of the business are the writers, the men and women who roam through the black neighborhoods collecting the dreams of black people in the form of "plays" that generally range from a dime to a dollar. The writers, at designated times, turn the bets and slips in to a station, or drop, which is most often the back room of a tavern or poolroom. Then a "runner" picks up the slips and bets (and the dreams) and takes them to the "clearing house" or "bank."

At the next level is the "baron" or "banker." In the black neighborhoods, he is nowadays usually a Negro; he is in charge of the clearing house and of that particular district. He directly oversees the "counters"— usually a corps of black women—who tally the wagers and slips (and dreams) and set aside the writer's commission, which is perhaps 15 percent of the amount he turns in. The baron is always a man of means and influence. He often controls a large amount of black votes, and he can fix a traffic ticket or minor beef. In some cases he can handle a "nigger-knifing" or "nigger-killing"; most likely, he has two or three "nigger-killings" to his own credit. He is seldom arrested. (But when the real heat is on, it is he or one of his chief lieutenants who goes to prison.)

At the head of the numbers operation is the shadowy "big man," who looms like a specter not only over the numbers game but over the entire neighborhood. He is the representative of an organized criminal syndicate which, according to some law officials, plucks an annual $6 billion out of the pocketbooks and dreams of black people. In return for this enormous sum, the "big man" and his invisible partners, through their political connections and with their hired guns, provide the baron and his subordinates with protection from the police and also from ambitious independent operators or young black men who might be bold enough to stick up a station or clearing house. (The threat of the syndicate's guns also insures that the banker and his subordinates do not "hold out" any of the take.) The "big man," often in partnership with the baron, has his fingers in other pies: crap games, narcotics, prostitution, loan-sharking—all of which suck the blood out of black neighborhoods.

The numbers operation with its blood-sucking corollaries could not exist without the aid and assistance of a corrupt political system whose bosses also grow fat off the dimes and dreams of black people. According to the *Report by the President's Commission on Law Enforcement and Administration of Justice*: "Today's corruption is less visible, more subtle and therefore more difficult to detect and assess than the corruption of the prohibition era. [But] All available data indicate that organized crime flourishes only where it has corrupted local officials. . . . To secure political power, organized crime tries by bribes or political contributions to corrupt the non-office holding political leaders to whom judges, mayors, prosecuting attorneys and correctional officials may be responsive."

In some neighborhoods there have been times in which the local political system was so corrupt that the "big man" could have policemen, ostensibly patrolling the neighborhood, guard the drops and clearing houses against stickup men. From time to time a writer or runner is arrested (especially before a local election) or a drop or clearing house is raided. The small fish are then fined or given short jail sentences. And there are times when federal officials intervene in the rackets and a baron—or one of his lieutenants—is arrested and sentenced to prison. But neither the "big man," the principals in the crime syndicate, nor the corrupt political officials are ever arrested and convicted of a crime.

When the real heat is on, say after a baron has been busted, a numbers operation may fold. But immediately another springs up, brandishing an exotic name—"Yellow Dog" or "Blue Angel" or "Bright Star." The demand for business is always great. The black people still have their dimes and their dreams, and the syndicate and the politicians still have their connections and their greed.

There is little doubt that the numbers games are an influence in the lives of many ghetto people. It is as common to hear a mother say, "I gotta get my number

in today," with the same concern — and sometimes in
the same breath — as she says, "I gotta feed the baby."
Men, on their way to and from work, play their numbers as regularly as they punch the time clock. Hustlers,
whores, deacons, and grandmothers, all play their favorite numbers. In some homes the "dream book" is
as familiar and is read with almost the same reverence
as the Bible.

And there are others, besides the organized criminals
and corrupt politicians, who live off the dreams of black
people. Along any main avenue of a black community
one can find, crammed in against the poolrooms, pawn-
shops, and storefront churches, a shop specializing in
lucky numbers, herbs, holy water, and "dream books"
(*Gypsy Queen, Aunt Mandy, Black Sal,* etc.). Negro
weekly newspapers carry advertisements by "prophets"
and "preachers," who, for a fee of course, will bless
numbers, interpret dreams, and prophesy "hits."

Some people argue the desirability of the numbers
game. Saul Alinsky, a nationally known community
organizer, has said that playing the numbers has been
one of the major ways that black people have sustained
their hopes over these many years of oppression. Others
argue that a numbers operation provides employment
for a group of people, that the "hits" stimulate the flow
of money in black neighborhoods, and that "people
will just naturally gamble."

Now, while there may be just a little truth to their
arguments, how do they measure the truth of the dreams
that are crumpled along with each slip or policy drawing that flutters in the gutter while the baron, the "big
man," and the greedy politicians glide by in their shiny
cars. The benefits to a black community from a numbers operation is a mouse's tit compared to the elephant's
udder suckled by the syndicate and politicians. And,
perhaps some scholar on the subject of the collective
dreams of an oppressed people could explain to those

who argue for the numbers operation why it is that three of the constantly played combinations are 6-6-60, 5-10-15, and 2-19-29, which, according to the dream books, are respectively sexual intercourse, clear water, and money. And also why the two most often played combinations of all are: 3-6-9 and 7-11-44. The former is shit; the latter is blood.

For Freckle-Faced Gerald

Now you take ol Rufus. He beat drums,
was free and funky under the arms,
fucked white girls, jumped off a bridge
(and thought nothing of the sacrilege),
he copped out—and he was over twenty-one.

Take Gerald. Sixteen years hadn't even done
a good job on his voice. He didn't even know
how to talk tough, or how to hide the glow
of life before he was thrown in as "pigmeat"
for the buzzards to eat.

Gerald, who had no memory or hope of copper hot lips—
of firm upthrusting thighs
to reenforce his flow,
let tall walls and buzzards change the course
of his river from south to north.

(No safety in number like back on the block.
two's aplenty. three? definitely not.
four? "you're all muslims."
five? "you were planning a race riot."
plus, Gerald could never quite win
with his precise speech and innocent grin
the trust and fists of the young black cats.)

Gerald, sun-kissed ten thousand times on the nose
and cheeks, didn't stand a chance,
didn't even know that the loss of his balls
had been plotted years in advance
by wiser and bigger buzzards than those
who now hover above his track
and at night light upon his back.

The Innocents

The story of innocent men, wrongly imprisoned, is an old one. It has been told in many books and movies, either showing a devoted mother who scrubs floors for years to prove her son's innocence, or showing a loyal wife, aided by a nonestablishment lawyer, struggling and finally proving that her innocent husband was the victim of misidentification. The most recent example of an innocent man regaining his freedom after years in prison is the case of Dr. Sam Sheppard.

Our prison here enjoys the queer distinction of having two Innocents. Neither man, however, is a Dr. Sam Sheppard or the like; both are poor and black. And they both prove the truths that Gunnar Myrdal stated over twenty years ago in *An American Dilemma:*

"American justice is everywhere expensive and depends too much upon the skill of the attorney. The poor man has difficulty in securing his rights . . . In matters involving offenses by Negroes against whites, Negroes will often find the presumptions of the courts against them, and there is a tendency to sentence them to a higher penalty than if they had committed the same offense against Negroes."

Now, to be sure, it is common to hear a convict say that he or another convict was "bum rapped." What he really means is that he feels that he or the other

convict was not convicted by due process of law, that
the other side — the Law — in the cops-and-robbers game
did not play the game according to the rules. But to
hear convicts who have lived with a man for years and
years say that that man is innocent is an altogether
different thing. Convicts are not easily fooled. Having
themselves, at one time or the other, employed the
many ruses and loopholes to beat the law, they are
quick to discern if a con is "playing the game" or if
he is "for real."

The largest segment of this prison's population is
made up of men who have been sentenced from Indianapolis, Indiana's largest city. Many of these men have
spent most of their adult lives traveling in and out of
this prison and the Indianapolis County Jail. Some
of them were in jail at the same time as the innocent
men; others have heard their attorneys or detectives,
especially Negro detectives, remark about these cases.
All these fragments form a picture. And also, there is
a kind of compulsion that drives a man to confess his
crime to somebody at some time or other. (The police
are well aware of and often take advantage of this fact
by planting a stool pigeon in a suspect's cell.) So, for
a convict to be deemed innocent, consistently, by a prison
population — where there are *no* secrets — is sometimes
the revelation of a truth that has not been brought out
by the "facts" presented in a court of law.

The following stories of the two Innocents here are
classical in their black-white sociolegal aspects. One
case is a so-called rape-kidnap of a white girl by six
black men (some of the guys here call the men "Indiana's
Scottsboro Boys"); the other case involves the misidentification of an innocent man by a white female robbery
victim.)

THE TROUBLES OF DONALD PECK

"I been down so long 'til down don' bother me" is
the first line from an old Blues; and it expresses ex-

actly how Donald Peck looks and acts after twenty years of imprisonment on a life sentence (along with four other men) for the supposed rape-kidnap. He is a slim coppery-colored man who seldom speaks; when he does, his voice is low and vague. Twenty years have eroded what was once perhaps gentleness or timidity into an insipidness that is reflected in his eyes, his gait, and in his slack face that still bears traces of his blown youth.

The troubles of Donald Peck began in 1947. As it was in cities the country over, 1947 was a turbulent year in Indianapolis, Indiana. Downtown, business boomed; factories, offices, and stores hummed and buzzed with the activities of the white boys, who, home from the wars, had hurled themselves into the "rat race," making up for lost time and money. Meanwhile, uptown, the black boys, home from the wars, found that nothing much had changed for them while they were away fighting for freedom. And disenchanted, disillusioned, unemployed and confused, a few of them in their pain had turned to the two new things that were then sweeping the avenues: heroin and be-bop. Many more of them turned to whiskey, wine and violence. Nineteen forty-seven, a turbulent year; the year that Donald Peck, then twenty-one, returned home to Indianapolis with an Honorable Discharge from the U. S. Navy tucked in his pocket.

One night in September of 1947, Peck met up with five men in a hang-out restaurant on one of the avenues in Indianapolis' black ghetto. Two of the men, Tommy L. Gardner, 22, and Stuart Derickson, 21, were also veterans of the U. S. Armed Forces. (Under circumstances which I will later relate, Derickson was released about three years after the other five had been sentenced to life.) The other three men in the hang-out were Robert Warner, 30, James Johnson, 20, and James Henderson, 25. They were recently released veterans of Indiana's State Reformatory.

"The night started out just like any other night," Tommy Gardner recalled. "I hadn't been in the place long. A bunch of us was just fucking around, bullshitting and listening to the music from the juke box."

Soon, it seems, somebody suggested whiskey. After the bottle had been bought and emptied, the six men piled into Tommy Gardner's car and set out to make the rounds.

"After we went to a few taverns," said Gardner, "I drove out south to a joint where a broad I knew worked. We sat around out there awhile, drinking and jiving, then we left, heading back north. We had decided to go to Anderson, Indiana. As I drove up Illinois Street, a gray pulled up beside me and shouted out of his car window, telling me to turn down my radio and calling us a bunch of names. Then he pulled off and I took off after him."

According to Gardner, the chase ended when the white man pulled up beside a police patrol car that had stopped for a red light. The man enlisted the aid of the two white policemen; and the policemen, according to Gardner, "chewed our asses out, took my license number, and told us to get our black asses off Illinois Street."

It is safe to say that such an incident is an ordinary and minor one in the lives of most black men in the United States; still, nobody knows what forces were set into motion in the minds and souls of the six men. What is known, though, is that they acted in one of the ways usual to a large number of black men when they are caught in a vortex of fear-hate-policemen-emasculating racism: they drove away and got drunker.

Donald Peck, who was a novice drinker, was soon slumped on the back seat of the car. The other men, veterans of the bottle, continued to drown their sorrows. The drinking lasted till around midnight.

"Finally," said Robert Warner, the oldest of the men, "we decided to call it a night and split. And as Tommy was driving us home, I happened to see this fay chick I knew, walking down the street with a fay sailor. I didn't know her personally but I'd seen her on the avenue, and the word was that she did a little hustling. So I asked the guys if they wanted to turn a trick with a white broad."

Except Peck, who was still slumped in the back seat of the car, and Tommy Gardner, all the men agreed to "turn a trick with a white broad." Gardner was instructed to pull over and park. Four men got out of the car: Robert Warner, James Johnson, James Henderson, and Stuart Derickson.

"I went to sleep under the wheel while they were gone," said Gardner. "When I woke up, they were back with this woman."

What occurred when the four men approached the woman and the sailor is unclear. Robert Warner said, "All I did was ask her if she wanted to make some money." James Johnson said, "I walked up, grabbed her by the arm and told her to come on." James Henderson said, "I didn't do anything, just walked up and looked." The sailor, the woman's boy friend of the moment, later testified at the trial that he didn't attempt to rescue the girl, "because I knew what kind of girl she was; and besides when this guy walked up and called her by her name, I felt she knew him. So when they told me to go on and mind my own business, I did. Still, when I turned to walk away, one of the men hit me on the head with his fist."

With the woman in the car the men drove out of the city into the dark countryside. For some strange reason, they first parked in some farmer's backyard, but the farmer shooed them off. They drove further into the country; and there, in a patch of woods, under a moon-filled night, four black men, or five, circled around one white woman . . .

When is rape not rape? When the act is committed

semipublicly, under the eyes of other men. It then becomes
a ceremony, a ritual. (Rapists in the usual sense are
loners, and their solitariness extends to all phases of
their lives; even in prison, their aloneness is more pro-
nounced than is that of other convicts.) Under what
circumstances do men commit openly before their brothers
an act which is essentially personal and private yet
which expresses most clearly their manhood, their selves?
Only when that manhood, that self, is threatened with
immediate extinction: Like in war, when soldiers, before
the battle, queue up to the whorehouses, or when, after
the battle, with the song of death still singing in their
brains, they ravish the women of the vanquished: Like
in critical times of a people when the act is exalted
in the dance or in religion to stimulate the life urge
of that people: Like when men live under soul-crushing
racism and feel that they must somehow, rightly or
wrongly, redeem and reassert themselves as men in
their own eyes and in the eyes of their brothers.

Even now, twenty years later, as four of the men
relate the story, one senses an ambivalence. On the one
hand there is the shame, the sorrow and the guilt; on
the other hand, there is an odd kind of self-esteem, a
statement of haughtiness that belies the shame, if not
the sorrow and guilt. And, as they relate their stories,
one notices too the lighted eyes, the twitching fingers,
the muscles tensing, as if they were once again, somewhere in their souls, acting out the deed. In some of
the listeners too, one senses a quiet tenseness. Because
the majority of the convicts have at one time or another
participated in, or witnessed, a "gang-bang," and because
some of them are familiar with the circumstances of the
crime, the involved men suffer no loss of status in the
prison pecking order, as do most men who are convicted
of sex crimes. This is true of all the men but Donald
Peck. He tells his story reluctantly, without any feeling
whatsoever; and, although his position is not that of

the common sex-criminal, he is often the object of tragi-comical remarks: "Just think, man — twenty years! — and he didn't even get none of the puss!"

That Donald Peck indeed had nothing to do with the so-called rape-kidnap of the white woman that night in the countryside over twenty years ago is verified by all the men involved.

"When I finished tricking with the broad," said James Henderson, "I shook Peck who was still knocked out in the back seat and asked him if he wanted to take care of the business. He sat up and looked around. I asked him again; and do you know what the guy said? He said, 'Naw, man, I ain't got no overcoat.'" [i.e., prophylactic — E. K.]

Peck had learned well the lessons in hygiene taught to him by the U. S. Navy. He sank back into his stupor, blotting out the white woman, the black men, the dark countryside.

The men finished with the woman and, according to Tommy Gardner, drove back to town. "I stopped at a streetcorner on the southside, but the woman wouldn't get out. She started arguing about the money. The guys wanted to give her ten dollars but she wanted fifteen. She finally got out of the car, still arguing, and said that if the sailor had said anything that she was going to have all of us busted for rape. When she said *that*, I told her I'd give her the other five bucks, but she said that she wasn't talking to me. By this time the other guys were getting hincty and cursing her, so I drove off."

Gardner drove the men home. Again, Donald Peck had to be roused, and this time escorted to his house by one of the men.

The sailor, it seems, had indeed said something. It was also later discovered that a woman, sitting in the doorway of her home, had seen "three colored boys force a white girl into a car" and reported it to the

police. The policemen who had earlier that night taken
Gardner's license number remembered the incident. And
the following night Gardner was arrested at his home
and charged with rape and kidnap. A few hours later
Robert Warner, whose picture was identified in the rogues'
gallery by the white woman, was also arrested and charged. All during the preliminary "interrogation" in the late
hours of the night at the police station, the two stead-
fastly denied the charges.

Donald Peck woke up on the morning of September 17,
1947, and read of the arrests in the newspaper. He
began to worry. Although the paper hadn't mentioned
his name or anything, he knew that he was mixed up
in that night's business, but he could not clearly recall
what had happened. He remembered enough, however,
to know that what had happened was not rape and
kidnap. "I told my mother," he said, "that I was going
downtown to the police and straighten things out." With
faith in American justice and loyalty to his friends,
Peck went downtown, and the police arrested him and
charged him too with rape and kidnap.

The three men were lodged in the county jail. Although
Peck had voluntarily surrendered himself, although he
had no previous police record whatsoever, his bond,
along with Gardner's and Warner's, was set at an excessively high figure, a sum impossible for him to raise.

During the first week of their incarceration, two major
crimes of violence by black men against whites occurred:
A white woman was raped and murdered by a black
man (Robert Austin Watts was later electrocuted for
this crime which is still controversial in black neighborhoods), and a white man was robbed and beaten to
death, allegedly by five black men. The newspapers
and radios screamed of "lawlessness and crime in the
streets" and called for a "crackdown and cleanup" cam-
paign. Citizens committees were formed; ambitious detectives and similarly motivated young deputy prose-

cutors made inflammatory and incriminating statements
to the press.

Robert Warner, having dealt previously with American
justice, saw which way the wind was blowing and decided to "cop a plea." The other men (all had been arrested by now) agreed that it was the best thing to do.
"After all, we were guilty of *something*," said Warner.
Peck, still loyal to his friends and still maintaining his
faith in American justice, also decided to "go along with
the program and take a share of the weight."

To cop a plea is to become involved in one of the
slipperiest aspects of the American judicial system: The
Negotiated Plea of Guilty. According to the *Report by
the President's Commission on Law Enforcement and
Administration of Justice,* released in February, 1967:
"Most defendants who are convicted — as many as 90
per cent in some jurisdictions — are not tried. They
plead guilty, often as the result of negotiations about
the charge or sentence. It is impossible to generalize
about the ways in which they are negotiated, so much
does practice vary from jurisdiction to jurisdiction. . .
[But] the two generalizations that can be made are that
when plea negotiations are conducted, they usually are
conducted out of sight, and that the issue in a plea
negotiation always is how much leniency an offender
will be given in return for a plea of guilty. . . . Usually
a prosecutor has considerable latitude as to what to
charge. Some sets of facts can be characterized as either
felonies or misdemeanors, or as crimes in the first,
second, or third degree. . . . *An obvious problem is
insuring that the defendant receives from the judge the
sentence he has bargained for with the prosecutor.* Under
existing practice, the fact negotiations have occurred is
commonly denied on the record, and so is the explicit
or tacit expectation that the judge will impose the agreed
punishment." [Emphasis added.]

Robert Warner, having already decided to cop a

plea, was nevertheless wary. His suspicions, as shall
be seen, were well founded. He had too many times
before seen men sold out, sometimes by their own defense counsel in collusion with the prosecutor. He sent
for his sister and his girl friend. In the presence of the
women, the detective assigned to the case, and a deputy
prosecutor, he copped out, signed statements admitting
to the crime, in exchange for a promise from the prosecutor of a 2 - 21 year sentence.

The other men followed suit.

"They wouldn't let us tell the whole truth, man," said
Robert Warner. "They wanted a conviction on all of
us. If we told them that Peck had nothing to do with
it, we'd all get life, they said."

In October of 1947, the six men went to be arraigned
in the Marion County (Indianapolis) Criminal Court.
Being poor and unable to retain private attorneys,
five of them were assigned defense counsel by the court.

(On the subject of the Public Defender or "pauper
attorney," the *Report by the President's Commission*
noted: "There are clear disadvantages to reliance on
the most common assignment system: the appointment
of counsel by the judge from among lawyers he happens
to know or who happen to be in the courtroom. This
leads to an unfair allocation of cases and sometimes,
when assigned counsel receive compensation from the
state, it is seriously abused." The community of criminal
lawyers in Indianapolis is known by those who require
its services as one of the worst in the country. Numerous
stories — many undoubtedly false — are told of attorneys
who have sold out small-fee clients in exchange for
some future favor from the prosecutors or from policemen. According to the *Report by the President's Commission*, ". . .In nearly every large city a private defense bar of low legal and dubious ethical quality can
be found. Few in number, these lawyers typically carry
large caseloads and in many cities dominate the practice

in routine cases. They frequent courthouse corridors, bondsmen's offices, and police stations for clients, and rely not on legal knowledge but on their capacity to manipulate the system. Their low repute often accurately reflects the quality of the services they render.")

Only *three* of these "pauper attorneys" were assigned to the *five* men who were charged with crimes for which they could, and did, receive life sentences.

So, in an atmosphere of racial hostility, created not only by the nature of the charges against them, but also because of the two crimes that had occurred since their arrest, the men went to trial on December 1, 1947. Having copped out and signed statements, they were resigned to sentences of 2-21 years. But they were in for a surprise. After all the parties connected with the matter were sworn, after the trial had begun — when the prosecutor was making his opening statement — then, and only then, did the men find out that they were being tried for both kidnap and rape; the former carried a life sentence, the latter carried the bargained-for 2-21 years.

All the men but Robert Warner were stunned. He demanded a halt to the trial, but to no avail. The three "pauper attorneys," after a feeble gesture of protest, swore they would "fight to the end" — despite the fact that they had held only *four* pretrial conferences with the men. To his credit, one attorney did try to call into question the allegedly raped woman's veracity by attempting to establish that she possessed a police record and had had four children by four different men, one of whom was black. But such points obviously and rightfully were not allowed for the all-white jury's consideration.

The accused men took the witness stand and swore that Donald Peck had nothing at all to do with the woman. The woman herself testified that Donald Peck had nothing to do with her, that he was in fact asleep in the car. But the all-white jury wasn't buying. After the prosecutor's fiery closing speech, *all five men* were convicted and sentenced to life.

(Stuart Derickson, the sixth man involved, was more fortunate. It seems that he had received a medical discharge from the army and was getting a $136 per month disability pension; also, his mother was able to raise some money. So Stuart Derickson hired a private attorney, had a separate trial, and was committed to the "Blue Walls," a mental institution that was then here at the prison. Three years later he was free. It is said that he spent $6,000. He has since then served a sentence in the reformatory for robbery; but in that connection there was no mention of his mental condition. One wonders what would have been the outcome of the trial if the other men had had the same amount of money.)

On December 3, 1947, James Johnson, James Henderson, Tommy Gardner, and Donald Peck were shackled and bound and delivered to the Indiana State Prison. The public was satisfied; for it, as well as for the three court-appointed attorneys, the story was ended, soon to be forgotten.

But for Donald Peck it was a new beginning. Warner, Johnson, and Henderson, it will be remembered, had previously "done time." So they soon "adjusted." But for Gardner and Donald Peck, prison was a horror — especially for Peck, not only because of his innocence, but also because of his youth, good looks, and timidity. He was made to order for the wolves. An old-timer, who was here when Peck came, said, "They passed him around like a beach ball." Twenty years have passed and he's still being passed around.

His spirit has been broken. From 1963 to this date he has not even bothered to petition to appear before the annual Clemency Board. (In Indiana, a man serving life becomes eligible for parole after ten years.)

All five of the men are still here. All of them have had clear prison records (if that proves anything) for at least the past ten years.

THE DILEMMA OF J. W. "ICEWATER" PREWITT

Unlike the quiet Donald Peck, in whom all the fire seems to have died, the other innocent man here is a raging volcano. The prison officials call him a "trouble-maker"; the old-timers say "he's doing hard time"; his friends counsel him to "be cool" while secretly admiring his spunk. (As I write this he's locked up for insubordination and writing love notes.)

J. W. "Icewater" Prewitt is 5 feet and 8 inches tall; he weighs 140 pounds. He is 26 years old, but with his beardless face and small stature he looks much younger. He has been in prison now for six years on a 10-25 year sentence for robbery which consisted of a purse snatching. He was born in Brownsville, Tennessee, but his parents, attracted by the World War II defense plants, moved to Indianapolis, Indiana, in 1942. Soon afterwards, his parents separated, and with his sister and two brothers, he grew up living first with one parent and then with the other.

His present troubles began in 1961. Conditions were no better then in the black neighborhoods after the Korean war than they had been after the Second World War. For some of the disinherited young men growing up in this period, added to the whiskey, wine, reefer, and heroin, was the "red devil" or "goof ball." With their hair processed (straightened) and tied up with "do-rags" to hold it in place, they would "down the red devils," gang fight, gang-bang the girls, swipe hot cars, and sometimes rob and assault, as they were swept along in the system's back currents — currents that would sweep them to an early death or to insanity or, more likely, to prison. The older generation on the corners called these young men "do-rag cats." J. W. Prewitt was a prince of the do-rag cats, and it was his do-rag that had a lot to do with his present troubles.

There seems to be a great deal of truth in the saying among black people that "to white folks all niggers look alike." Take two young black men of the same general description and then cover their heads with similar colored do-rags; take one frightened white woman who has been beaten and robbed in the middle of the night, and you have a fifty percent chance of the wrong man being identified as the robber. Like in Prewitt's case.

According to Prewitt, it all started on Friday, June 16, 1961: "I was standing on the street corner of Twenty-third and Illinois Street. It was about five-thirty in the morning, when a police cruiser pulled up to the curb. The officers asked me my name which I'm sure that they already knew. I told them my name; I told them that I was waiting on a friend of mine, Anthony Howard, who with my sister had just gone home to see if he could borrow his father's car. The officer who remained in the car called the police headquarters while the other officer searched me. I then heard the dispatcher at the police headquarters tell the policemen to bring me in.

"When I arrived at police headquarters, I was taken to the detective's division. Two white detectives interviewed me. I asked them what had I been arrested for, and they just avoided answering. They seemed more concerned in asking me if I was a junkie. They said that they had heard that I was on dope. In closing their conversation they said that if I got sick they would charge me with being a common addict. The next day, Saturday, I appeared before the police line-up, and the officer there said I had been seen hanging out on the northside. Sunday nothing happened. Monday morning, when I went to preliminary court, the two detectives asked that my case be continued for seven days. I was then carried to the county jail."

I first met Prewitt when he entered the county jail. I remember it well because, even as the jailers were ushering him into the cell block, he was raising hell, screaming his innocence. I was "cell boss" at the time (which is another story), and during the months spent together awaiting trial, we became close friends. Within hours after he was in jail he was in a fight (which he lost). But because of his "game" spirit, his readiness to fight *anybody* despite his small size and youth, he was soon adopted as a kid brother by the clique of older men (myself included) that ran the cellblock.

From one point of view he profited from this adoption; he was in jail; he had to survive. On the other hand, while he survived, he formed habits that he has not yet broken. In the Indianapolis County Jail in 1961, a young man — unless was extremely unattractive — had two choices: to ride or to be ridden. Prewitt chose to ride. And during the months spent in jail, when he was not shouting his innocence to anyone who would listen, he — along with others — was venting his anger and frustration through sexual advances on other less strong young men. (At the time he was only twenty, but he looked fifteen. And his fearlessness and/or coldness that contrasted so sharply with his youthful face soon earned him the nickname of "Icewater." The nickname has stuck with him for these six years, and so have the fearlessness and anger which he now mainly expresses toward the prison officials and abstract society. "Man," he has said, "I ain't done a motherfucking thing to be here, so why should I go along with anything these people say?")

As the days passed in the county jail in 1961, Prewitt began to make court appearances. But first he was fingered.

"Me and about five other guys were lined up," he said.

"And the deputy sheriff opened the door and in came a heavy-set white woman and one of the white detectives. The woman looked around for about five minutes and then her and the detective whispered something. The lady looked around for about five more minutes and then went into another whispering conference with the detective. Then she was sent out, and all the guys in the line-up were excused and sent back to the cellblock. I was asked to remain. Then this detective said, 'We have got you this time.' I asked him what was he talking about, and he said that the woman identified me as robbing her. I told him that she had to be mistaken and for him to have her take another look. He said that it wasn't necessary. I then told him that I would like to have a lie-detector test; he said that it wasn't necessary either and that I would be gone for a long, long time. I told him to go fuck himself.

"In the usual amount of time I was taken to court and arraigned. My mother had hired a white attorney, William C. Erbecker. My plea was not guilty, and I was told that my case would be scheduled. Before my trial was scheduled my lawyer decided to present a writ of *habeas corpus* to get my bond reduced. [Although the *habeas corpus* is, in theory, a writ requiring that a prisoner be brought before the court to decide the legality of his detention, it is seldom used as such in Indianapolis. — E. K.] My lawyer told me that I would have to file a Statement of Alibi in the writ telling where I was the night of the crime, Monday, June 12, 1961, which was four days before I was arrested.

"At the hearing of the *habeas corpus*, my Statement of Alibi was presented into evidence. The statement was that on the night of the crime I was at the house of a friend, Frank Starks, with another friend, Anthony Howard, the guy I was waiting on when I was arrested; that we all had left my house that Monday evening and were at this friend's house drinking beer and watching television all evening and most of the night until, full of beer, we all went to sleep. The state's witness wasn't able to attend the hearing, so the detectives said, and they objected to a bond reduction. The judge went along with them, as I knew he would.

"In January of 1962, my trial was set; I don't remember the exact date. While the jury was being selected, I noticed that out of almost a hundred prospective jurors only about three were black. I asked the attorney if I could get some colored people on my jury. Mr. Erbecker told me that if I didn't feel that I was going to get a fair trial that I should tell the judge. A recess was called and I asked the judge if I could have some colored people on my jury. The judge told me that he would see to me getting a fair and impartial trial. I then asked him if it wasn't my constitutional right to have some colored people on my jury. He told me that the only thing necessary was that discrimination wasn't used in summoning the prospective jurors. I guess he was right about that. But what twelve white people are going to believe two or three black men in a court where the judge is white, the prosecutor is white, and the defense attorney is even white? The prosecutor and my lawyer then proceeded in the game of picking twelve unbiased white people.

"Things happened during my trial that I had not throught possible. This white woman sat in the witness chair, under oath, pointed at me and said that I was the one who had robbed her. She put on an unbelievable act. She went on to say how she remembered every scar on my face, the way my hair was processed and everything about me. Emphasis was placed on how she went to the hospital after the brutal purse snatching. With the aid of the prosecutor, she was spewing out all these lies and all the while looking directly at me.

"The state then introduced a shirt that was torn to shreds. During the struggle over the purse they said that this blue, summer-type shirt was supposed to have been torn off the attacker.

"As my trial went on, I began to sense that my white attorney wasn't acting in my behalf. I told him that he wasn't doing anything but allowing lies to be told on me. My mother, who has a dreadful fear of white people, probably because of her Southern upbringing and the fact that she's uneducated, continuously demanded that I 'hush up.' During one of the recesses I asked her to dismiss the attorney but she refused to."

The description Prewitt gives of his conduct in the courtroom is questionable. Other jail inmates who had witnessed the trial as they waited to be tried themselves gave a different version when they were brought back to jail. "Man," one of them said, "that Icewater is pitching a bitch over there. The way he's acting they're going to throw the book at him." Another man said, "Icewater tried to fire his lawyer in the middle of the trial. . . . And he told the judge, the prosecutor, and everybody in the jury that they were all prejudiced and that that woman was lying. They're gonna sock it to 'im."

Whenever Prewitt was brought back to the cellblock during the recesses in his trial, the older men (myself included) would urge him to stop acting up, to go along with his lawyer and maybe he would beat the case. It was obvious that he had not yet grasped a major facet of American justice, as it is applied to black people: that even if you are right, you have to be right in a certain manner. Each time that he'd leave the cellblock to return to the courtroom, I— and other friends of his— would caution him to be cool, to hang tough; and each time, he'd remark: "They're lying, so fuck 'em."

The trial went on. In his words: "The state continued to introduce their evidence. A detective sergeant took the witness stand and stated that he had another witness to the crime, but that she was unable to appear in court. This was the same detective sergeant who had accompanied the woman at the line-up at the county jail. I'm more than sure that he is the one who picked me out and influenced the woman during the whispering conferences. My attorney brought out the fact that this detective had been disciplined by his board of captains, or something like that, for lying.

"The next thing that I learned at the trial was how my name became involved. The only colored officer in the case took the stand. He explained how two days after the crime, he had taken four mug shots by the woman's house and she picked out mine. I now realize that she is the caliber of woman who would have picked one of those pictures, as long as it was a colored guy with processed hair and a do-rag on.

"The next witness to take the stand was a police sergeant, with over fifteen years on the force. He was the one who was supposed to have placed me within the vicinity of the crime. He stated that he saw me on the night of the crime in a car, driving down Northwestern Avenue. He was asked by my defense attorney to pick out my mug shot. *He picked out the wrong picture right there in court.* [Emphasis added. This was also loudly verified by other jail inmates who witnessed the trial and also by a deputy sheriff who took Prewitt to court. The police officer had picked the picture of another youth, a do-ragger, who was then in jail on a car-theft.— E. K.] My attorney brought out that this policeman had been in this type of work for over fifteen years and sitting right across from me he could not pick the right mug shot. It was then brought out that my brother, Willie, was driving down Northwestern on that particular night and had received a speeding ticket in that area, which the traffic records can show.

"My attorney put Frank Starks on the stand. He is the friend whose house I stayed at the night the crime took place. He testified to that, just like I had told them almost six months earlier in the Statement of Alibi.

"Then it was thought that the trial would have to be

continued for a couple of days to figure out how to get
my other witness to court. He was now in the U. S.
Air Force, stationed in Texas. My lawyer suggested to
my mother to get plane fare and send it to him. My
mother borrowed some money and sent for Anthony
Howard. He arrived the next day and gave the same
testimony that had been given earlier, but the prosecutor confused him on whether or not there was a television in the apartment. I had not been in communication with Anthony since I had been arrested,
but if I had known that I was going to have to go
through all this, I would have made damn sure that he
knew every piece of furniture in Frank Starks' house.
My lawyer asked me if I wanted to take the stand. I
said yes."

Prewitt's attitude on the witness stand, according to
others, was definitely not designed to solicit the jury's
sympathy.

"I took the stand," he said, "and the prosecutor asked
me if I would try on the torn shirt. I said sure. After
manipulating the shirt for a few minutes it appeared
to be my size. The prosecutor also brought out that
I had been arrested for robbery before and that I had
received six months on the State Penal Farm for auto
theft. He didn't mention that I was innocent of that
robbery charge too.

"To sum up my trial, the state introduced one witness,
the victim, and a shirt that fitted me, like any shirt of
that size would. My alibi, which also happened to be
the truth, was proved, except for Anthony Howard
being unsure of whether a television was in the apartment or not. Even though the judge instructed the jury
to take into consideration that I had proved my alibi,
it only took the all-white jury a little over eight hours
to return a guilty verdict. Everybody in the courtroom
put on a big act of surprise, including my lawyer—
who was fired after it was too late. But I knew from

the beginning that I was going to be convicted. What all-white jury is going to take the words of three black men over the word of one white woman?

"I was taken back to jail to await pre-sentence investigation for probation, which I knew I wasn't going to get. For the first time in my life I had nightmares and became so unable to sleep that my skin began to feel like it was crawling. One day as I was talking about how unbelievable it was that a woman could lie so boldly, a guy that I had been knowing for many years asked me where had this crime happened at. I told him, and this guy proceeded to tell me things that it was impossible for anyone to know unless he was in the courtroom during my trial or had had something to do with the crime. . . ."

Until this time, I—along with many others in jail—had not really taken Prewitt's story of his innocence seriously. Of course we all had hoped that he would "beat" his charge, but knowing him and his groove at the time, I felt that he was quite capable of having committed the crime, and that he probably did. However, the man referred to in the above paragraph, whom I shall call here Curtiss Oldham, changed my mind.

One day, just before Prewitt's trial ended, Oldham came to my cell. He too was a young do-rag cat, and he had something on his mind. Since I was not only "cell boss" but also father-confessor and jailhouse lawyer, I thought at first that he wanted to talk about his own case; but he wanted to know how I thought Prewitt's case was going to turn out. When I told him that I thought Prewitt was uptight, he became more thoughtful. Finally he said, "Man, Icewater didn't do that; I did it." We talked. And there, in the presence of two other men (part of the clique), he told his story. I understood that by telling us he was obliquely seeking advice. He was caught between the code of "taking his own weight" and his desire for freedom. More than that, he and Prewitt were friends; likely as not they had swiped hot cars or robbed together. He said, "Damn, man, I sure hope Icewater beats the beef. I wish there was some way I could help him, but I can't just cop out to it and let 'em give *me* that ten to twenty-five. I'm gonna beat this beef I'm in here on now."

Everybody in the cell was silent for a while. We all understood Oldham's problem but we couldn't advise him to cop out — although we were now convinced that Ice water really was innocent. One may have friends in a county jail, but Damon and Pythias are unknown; to "look out for number one" is the order of the day. None of us older men would have *even considered* admitting to a crime to save a friend. But the do-rag cat did.

Prewitt, however, was determined that Oldham should take his own weight. He sent for Lieutenant Spurgeon Davenport, a Negro detective who was boss of the Homicide and Robbery Division of the Indianapolis police.

In Prewitt's words: "I told Lieutenant Davenport about this guy's statements and knowledge of my case, and the lieutenant decided to talk to this guy. And before he left the jail he said that he was going to look into my case. A few days later, Lt. Davenport summoned me across the street to police headquarters and told me that he had talked to every police official involved in my case. He said that a lot of the victim's testimony was doubtful, such as her statements that she remembered every scar on my face. He said that during a crime of this type there is too much fear involved to notice scars, and at night too. He also said that this guy in jail definitely knew a lot about the crime. In closing he told me that he was going to keep my case in mind."

Prewitt's pre-sentence investigation for probation ended. And on March 9, 1962, at the age of nineteen or twenty he was taken to the Indiana State Reformatory to serve a 10-25 year sentence.

"On entering the reformatory," he said, "I was asked if I wanted to donate my suit to the Salvation Army. I quickly told the guard that I did not, that I had been poor far too long, and that I had a brother who was still poor. I had my suit sent home. Within a few days I almost entered solitary confinement because I refused to sign a statement stating that I had been legally sentenced to the reformatory. Only when the paper was rewritten, stating clearly that I said I was innocent, did I sign it. After going through the quarantine stage, I was taken before the classification committee where an incident happened that made me say damn the hunky church forever. The chaplain who sat on the committee found it funny when I said that my mother was trying to raise $1,900 to get me a new trial. This man of God, laughing, said that for $2,000 I could get out next week. After the comedy routine was over, I was assigned to the powerhouse."

In April of 1962, also having received a 10-25 year sentence, I followed Prewitt to the reformatory. (Two days before I left the jail, Curtiss Oldham had beaten his case and gone to the streets.) After I got out of quarantine, I told Prewitt about Oldham's release. He took it badly. We were tight and spent a lot of time together. He was quieter, more sober, than he had been in jail. He had been in the Hole only once, a two-week stretch for threatening to kill a 200-pound, 35-year-old white man who owed him some cigarettes.

The summer of 1962 passed. There were no new developments in his case. His mother was struggling to pay the newly hired attorney to appeal his sentence. This attorney had talked to him only once and that was before he had left the county jail.

In February of 1963, I was transferred to the Michigan City State Prison. I was not to see Prewitt again until 1965 when he too was transferred to the prison here, but until then, the grapevine kept me informed. Curtiss Oldham, it seems, had been arrested again and was sentenced to the reformatory on another charge. Prewitt's conduct was deteriorating. He was back in the sex bag. He was fighting, arguing with the guards, staying high off "raisin jack" and pep pills, and generally raising hell.

In his words he tells of those months: "Almost a year and a half had passed since I had entered the reformatory before I had my first fight. The institution informers notified the officials and the guy and I were placed in solitary confinement. For the second time I was naked on the concrete floor, eating one-half meal a day. Before I got out of the Hole, an officer came to my cell one day and told me that I had a visitor. I got dressed; I thought it was my mother and sister.

"When I entered the visiting room, I was directed to a small partitioned-off room. In the room were Lt. James Dabner of the Indianapolis Police Department and a lieutenant from the Marion County (Indianapolis) Prosecutor's Office. They asked me a whole lot of questions about my case. They also took statements from the guilty guy's partner who drove the car. This accomplice was at the reformatory too. Before the Prosecutor's lieutenant and Lt. Dabner left, they told me that it was their job to get the innocent out as well as to put the guilty in. I felt pretty good.

"The very next day, I got a visit from my mother and sister. They told me that they had been notified by the Indianapolis police department that I was innocent, that the guilty party had been found, and that I would be coming home soon. I laughed and told them that I already knew all that. This happened in August or September of 1963."

It seems that the hopeful sparks soon fizzled out. Prewitt's new attorney had wanted at first to wait for the Indiana Supreme Court's ruling on Prewitt's old appeal for a new trial, but he decided to file a writ of *habeas corpus*. The writ was filed in Madison County, the county in which the reformatory is located. In November of 1963, Prewitt was taken to Anderson, Indiana, to appear in Superior Court. At the *habeas corpus* hearing, the Deputy Attorney General argued that the only question involved was whether or not Prewitt was being illegally held. He also argued that Madison County did not have the authority to rule on the evidence because Prewitt was sentenced to the reformatory from Marion County. He then innocently pointed out to the judge that Indiana had, just the past September, abolished the writ of error *coram nobis*, which was the only form of writ that could bring a defendant back to the county he was sentenced from. All the while, members of the police department and Prewitt's attorney were present, waiting to introduce the "new evidence." The presiding judge continued the case, and Prewitt was returned to the reformatory.

Four months later, the judge ruled that it was out of Madison County's jurisdiction to hear the new evidence. The judge, in effect, ruled that although Prewitt may indeed be innocent, wrongfully imprisoned, he was not illegally imprisoned. During the same time Prewitt learned that the Supreme Court had denied his old appeal. His lawyer began to lag on the case (and was later fired). His mother's money ran out. He heard no further word from the policemen who were supposed to be investigating his case.

Prewitt's conduct worsened; but he still screamed his innocence. He and his mother wrote letters to Bar Associations, to Legal Aid Societies, to state and federal officials. The federal people claimed "no jurisdiction"; the local people ignored him. He even wrote to the Vice-President and to Senator Robert F. Kennedy.

"About fifteen months had gone by," Prewitt said, "since the police had had the proof of my innocence. But I was still at the reformatory. I began to ignore what I called the hunky savages, the officials, and I was constantly being carried to solitary. I went from job to job; the redneck screws and I couldn't get along.

"I began to demand that some of the racist policies which flourished at the reformatory be ended. I purposely infuriated some of the guards by letting it be known that I had many young white homosexuals. [It might be significant to note here that Prewitt has since told me that one of the "white kids" was one of two youths who were convicted and sentenced to 1-10 years for a purse snatching which resulted in the woman's death by heart attack.] I made many I-don't-give-a-damn scenes with my little white kids. Sometimes I'd enter the cellhouse and just to see the screw's face turn red, I'd shout out that I was going down the range to kiss my little blue-eyed white girl. Many attempts were made to have me removed from the cellhouse, but there was no place to put me. I had already been in every cellhouse and dormitory then allowed to colored."

And so it went.

In 1965, because of his conduct, he was transferred here to the State Prison. He had not quite reached his twenty-fifth birthday. I myself was on the "rock" at the time, but as soon as I got off, we met on the yard. He had lost none of his fire.

He has been here for two years now; and he has constantly maintained (loudly) that he is innocent, while constantly staying in trouble with the officials. I have tried to point out to him that he has served enough time to make parole, and that he should try to keep his time clear so that he can go home where he'll have a better chance to prove his innocence. I have also pointed out to him that the State is by its nature reluctant to admit and rectify its mistakes; and since the state officials already suspect collusion between him and Oldham, the State is apt to put pressure on Oldham. But Prewitt listens (perhaps rightfully) to nothing. He is still fighting. And if he is "playing the game," he has for six years fooled not only me but the entire black populations of two prisons.

What is going to happen to him? Well, if he keeps in his same groove, he is likely to wind up at the mental institution. There, they will attach little electrodes to his head and blot out his brain.

From his conduct, one of two things is clear: either he IS innocent or he has a mental hangup. If he is innocent, why is he here? If he is sick, who or what made him so? One other thing — perhaps the most important — is outstandingly clear: He has said NO to the whole system.

Hard Rock Returns to Prison from the Hospital for the Criminal Insane

Hard Rock was "known not to take no shit
From nobody," and he had the scars to prove it:
Split purple lips, lumped ears, welts above
His yellow eyes, and one long scar that cut
Across his temple and plowed through a thick
Canopy of kinky hair.

The WORD was that Hard Rock wasn't a mean nigger
Anymore, that the doctors had bored a hole in his head,
Cut out part of his brain, and shot electricity
Through the rest. When they brought Hard Rock back,
Handcuffed and chained, he was turned loose,
Like a freshly gelded stallion, to try his new status.
And we all waited and watched, like indians at a corral,
To see if the WORD was true.

As we waited we wrapped ourselves in the cloak
Of his exploits: "Man, the last time, it took eight
Screws to put him in the Hole." "Yeah, remember when he
Smacked the captain with his dinner tray?" "He set
The record for time in the Hole—67 straight days!"
"Ol Hard Rock! man, that's one crazy nigger."
And then the jewel of a myth that Hard Rock had once bit
A screw on the thumb and poisoned him with syphilitic spit.

The testing came, to see if Hard Rock was really tame.
A hillbilly called him a black son of a bitch
And didn't lose his teeth, a screw who knew Hard Rock
From before shook him down and barked in his face.
And Hard Rock did *nothing*. Just grinned and looked silly,
His eyes empty like knot holes in a fence.

122

And even after we discovered that it took Hard Rock
Exactly 3 minutes to tell you his first name,
We told ourselves that he had just wised up,
Was being cool; but we could not fool ourselves for long,
And we turned away, our eyes on the ground. Crushed.
He had been our Destroyer, the doer of things
We dreamed of doing but could not bring ourselves to do,
The fears of years, like a biting whip,
Had cut grooves too deeply across our backs.

Inside These Walls

Prison legend has it that D. C. Stephenson, during the time that he was Grand Dragon of the Indiana Ku Klux Klan and a high-up in the state's politics, made a tour of the prison here and, finding the height of the walls not to his satisfaction, demanded that they be built higher "for the protection of society." Ironically, D. C. Stephenson, a few years later, found himself behind those newly heightened walls. He had been convicted of murder.

Today the walls of the Indiana State Prison are forty-three feet high; they are gray stone and concrete, surrounding twenty-three acres of land.

Inside these walls are 2,000 men, black, white, and brown, ranging in age from sixteen to eighty-three. The average age is thirty-six. The prison boasts one ex-policeman, one ex-Justice of the Peace, a bank embezzler, and four college graduates. The vast majority, however, come from the lower economic level and are small-time burglars, stickup artists, and forgers. Lifers make up the largest group; there are 450.

And what do these men do inside these walls? It's simple, maddeningly simple: At six o'clock in the morning a whistle blows. They get up and wash their faces. At six-fifteen, a bell rings, and they march off to the prison mess hall and eat a breakfast of, say, oatmeal, prunes, bread and coffee. They leave the mess hall in a line and drop their spoons in a bucket by the door, watched over by a "screw." They march to their shops — say the Tag Shop, climb upon a stool and dip license plates into a tank of paint until nine-thirty. A bell rings; they smoke. A bell rings; they go back to work.

At eleven-thirty, a bell rings again. They stop work, wash up, march back to their shelters. At twelve o'clock, a bell rings in the cellhouse; they walk to the mess hall where they eat, say, a meal of white beans, frankfurters, and cornbread. They leave the mess hall, drop their spoons into the bucket and, in line, go back to work. The morning performance is repeated. At four-thirty a whistle blows; they march to supper and then into their cellhouse for the night. Maddeningly simple.

Most of the ancient buildings in which the men work and live are made of red bricks, with green tile roofs. They rise stark and bare, ornamented only with steel-barred windows, deep-set and elongated windows that make the sides of the building look like sad-faced clowns. There are four cellhouses: A, B, C, and D; and two dormitories: I and G. Each cellhouse shelters approximately 400 men, and the two dormitories about 400.

One of the oldest and most famous cellhouses is "B" (BCH). It was built in 1907 and was once the home of John Dillinger. The first thing that strikes you about the cellhouse is its immensity. An oblong, barnlike building, it stretches more than two-thirds of a city block, and the glaring light bulbs strung along the walkways in front of the cells give the illusion of even greater distance. The cells are stacked five tiers high, ranging back to back down the center of the cellhouse with their fronts gaping at the outer walls.

Coming in from work, the men file up the iron stairs like long lines of worker ants, their heavy steps unlike the sounds made by any other group of moving men. As they reach their respective tiers, they break off, and each man goes to his cell. A bell rings twice, and at the front end of each gallery a guard begins to lock the cells and count the men. Then it is quiet time, nervous time, until after mail call, which will occur in about thirty minutes.

The cells are ten feet long and six feet wide. (Although the practice has been discontinued, two men were once assigned to some of these cells.) On the door of each cell is a card, bearing the inmate's name, number, and job assignment. Each cell contains a toilet bowl, a wash basin, a cot, a set of earphones, and whatever small furniture the inmates can either make or scrounge. For the past few years the men have been permitted to paint their own cells, choosing their own colors. Some men keep their cells extraordinarily neat. Precise. Others barely manage to pass the occasional inspection by the cellhouse officer. By and large a man is allowed to arrange his cell as he sees fit.

And what do the men do in their cells? One young man, a muscle boy, is doing push-ups. Two hundred a night. Another man is answering a letter that he has just received. One man is pacing his cell, stopping every now and then to crack his knuckles. Another is lying on his bunk listening to his earphones. Another is standing, gripping the bars and calling down the gallery to his buddy. Another is already in bed, his knees drawn up toward his chest, his blanket pulled over his head. Most of the men read books: Westerns, blood and sex detective mysteries, Gothic romances, and current book-list novels, in that order.

Some men have lived in the same cells for eight, ten, twelve years. The pressures are heavy, and the sounds made at night by 400 caged men are lonely and empty. A clacking typewriter, a flushing toilet, a futile curse, and drifting, distorted music from a radio. An inmate spends from fourteen to sixteen hours a day in his cell. Soon it becomes, in truth, his home.

Prison guards

The primary function of prison, some say, is to isolate and punish the criminal, and to that end we have the typical prison guard.

The pay for being a prison guard is about the same as that earned by a dishwasher in a large hotel. Why then do men become prison guards? Some, the majority, simply drift into the job. They are for the most part unskilled and semiliterate; ex-farmers, factory 'workers, common laborers, and the like. Others, a very small minority, are sexually perverted and would take any kind of job, just so long as it is around a large number of men over whom they have near total power. (It is these men and their inmate counterparts — and sometimes lovers — who are the causes of almost all cases of brutality in prison.) There is still another microscopic group who become keepers of men. They are the do-gooders, the humanitarians. They do not last long; or if they do last and gain positions of power, their efforts are nullified by politics, public apathy, and subversion by the men with whom they have to work.

Generally, prison guards are just plain, poor men. It is the nature of the work that brings out the worst in the best of them. Most of them are not equipped mentally, spiritually, or morally to work in the swamp of brutality, loneliness, sexual depravity, and scheming without themselves being covered with the same muck. A prison guard does time and, as with the inmate, it weighs heavily on his shoulders. Two years ago, a guard, on night duty in a gun tower on the wall, phoned Center Control and said, "I quit." Then he simply walked out of the gun tower, across to the parking lot, and drove away.

Because of the low pay some guards are easily bribed to smuggle contraband inside the prison. And because of their own positions in the world, or a nagging wife, or approaching sexual impotence, some guards succumb

to the insidious bootlicking and "brown-nosing" of favor-
currying inmates and become petty tyrants who are ma-
nipulated by these inmates for their, the inmates', own pur-
poses. Indeed, the competence of prison guards can be
measured in direct proportion to the number of "rats"
and bootlickers within a prison. Men have lost their
"clear time" — their chance to go home — on the uncorro-
borated word of another inmate.

It is not uncommon to hear two old-timers, one of
them a guard, talking longingly about the good old
days when the "joint was a joint." The guard, after long
years, is perhaps by now a lieutenant or a captain;
and he is not about to relinquish an iota of prerogative
or power to those "mother-coddling treatment guys."
Such guards have been known to enlist the aid of their
old buddy convicts in their fight.

There is still talk of the beatings and killings that
once occurred here: of the "water cure," of the soap-filled
cane, and of the "wrecking crew." Only a few years ago
skeletons were unearthed where the infamous "Blue Wall"
once stood. (The Blue Wall was the inmates' name for
the Hospital for the Criminal Insane that was once
inside the prison here.)

Physical brutality in prison, however, has, except for
a few isolated cases, gone by the board. Nowadays
a prison guard can be suspended or fired for striking
an inmate — unless, of course, it is in self-defense or in
the defense of another guard or an inmate.

Force has never proved to be an effective method
for controlling men, and prison officials have come to
realize this. For some reason, brutality and loose discipline in prison seem bound together; and too, there
seems to be a relationship between brutality and the
quality of the prison guards. Recently a new policy
relating to discipline was instituted here. The Hole and
other extreme forms of punishment were abolished —
and there has been no breakdown in normal order. The

fact is that physical brutality is as nothing compared to the brutality of the soul incurred by years and years of cancerous prison life.

Below is a copy, in the exact wording and punctuation, of a recently issued bulletin, setting forth the new policy:

OFFICE OF THE DEPUTY WARDEN
October 12, 1967

TO: Whom it may concern
CONCERNING: Conduct Adjustment Committee Policies [called the Kangaroo Court by the cons — E. K]

Effective this date a copy of the Conduct Adjustment Committee results will be forwarded to all shelters. This procedure will insure that all supervisory officers, as well as shelter officers, are fully acquainted with the Committee's actions, and therefore able to comply with the wishes of the Committee. It will be the responsibility of the shelter officers to keep these reports in a secure place at all times. Captains and Lieutenants will check the files periodically for compliance.

For the information of everyone (Officers and Inmates), the following policies and/or procedures are hereby announced, and are effective as of this date.

MAJOR OFFENSES: Some examples of offenses included in this category are:

1. Escape or Attempted Escape.
2. Fighting.
3. Contraband (Possession of Weapon, Knife, etc.)
4. Drunk.
5. Assaulting or threatening an officer.
6. Assaulting or threatening an inmate.
7. Sex offenses, also Obscene Literature and Pictures in the nude.
8. Unauthorized Medication.
9. Insolence (some instances).
10. Inciting a riot.

11. Gambling.
12. Unauthorized Alteration of clothing (some instances).
13. Destroying State Property (some instances).

MINOR OFFENSES: Some offenses included in this category are:
1. Out of place. [Being caught someplace without proper authorization — E. K.]
2. Contraband (food, etc.)
3. Bucking chow lines.
4. Refusing to obey orders.
5. Refusing job assignment.
6. Failure to comply with shelter rules.
7. Insolence (some instances).
8. Smoking in line.
9. Destroying State Property (some instances).
10. Loud or boisterous talk.
11. Refusing to work.
12. Unauthorized alteration of clothing (some instances).

Please be advised that the above listing of offenses for which an inmate may be brought before the Conduct Committee is not intended to be all inclusive, but rather as an example. In all cases the final decision as to whether an offense is considered minor or major, rests with the Committee.

DISCIPLINARY ACTIONS OF THE CONDUCT ADJUSTMENT COMMITTEE: Cases will normally be disposed of by utilizing one or more of the following procedures. Again this is only intended to serve as a guide for all concerned and final decision rests with the committee in all cases.

a. REPRIMAND: Verbal correction or reproof.

b. LOSS OF RECREATION: Locked in personal cell at all times except for hours spent on the job. Inmate may also leave his cell for purpose of going to and from work, the dining room, church, and visits. No other exceptions will be made.

c. COMPLETE LOSS OF PRIVILEGES: Locked in personal cell at all times except for movement to and from dining room, hospital, and visits. No further exceptions will be made. When moving to and from the hospital or visits, inmate must be escorted by an officer. Commissary is restricted to 2nd Grade [See Commissary List — E. K.] ONLY for the duration of this disciplinary action. Men sheltered in dormitory or I-Cellhouse will be moved to the Idle Shelter upon receiving disciplinary action of this nature. Upon completion of the penalty assessed by the Committee, a return transfer to the dormitory or I-Cellhouse, if appropriate, will be effected. Repeated offenses may result in permanent loss of opportunity to shelter in either the dormitory or I-Cellhouse. Men who have been assessed Complete Loss of Privileges will not be allowed a change in job or shelter, other than to the Seclusion Unit [Called the "Rock" — E. K.], during the period of time involved in the disciplinary action.

d. PLACEMENT IN 2nd GRADE: Men placed in 2nd Grade will lose the privileges of recreation, movies, club functions, and all related activities for a period of ninety (90) days. Commissary is restricted to 2nd Grade Items ONLY for the entire period. Loss of clear time.

e. WEEK END LOCK UP: Inmates receiving this disciplinary action will report to the Deputy's Office immediately after work on Friday for confinement in the Seclusion Unit. Release from Confinement will be effected in time to report to work on the following Monday morning.

f. BULL PEN TIME: For certain minor offenses reported on either Incident or Conduct reports, bull pen time, not to exceed two hours without a break, may be designated.

g. MAJOR OFFENSES: Offenses in this category may result in indefinite periods of confinement in the Seclusion Unit plus loss of good time and/or clear time, where the welfare of the individual or the population in general is concerned.

h. I-CELLHOUSE AND DORMITORY PRIVILEGES: A major offense will automatically cause the inmate to be removed from either of these shelters for a period of one year from the date of the offense. Two minor reports in a twelve month period will also constitute cause for removal from these shelters for one year. In this instance, eligibility date for return to one of the shelters will be one year from date of the last offense.

For your information it will be the Committee's prerogative to suspend all or any portion of any disciplinary action assessed by the committee. In cases where violation of the above policies occur, extensions of assessments in effect or new assessments will be imposed by the Committee. In all cases except the 2nd Grade ninety day period described above, duration of time involved in disciplinary actions will vary and will be determined on the merits of the individual case. Shelter Officers are charged with the responsibility of ascertaining if new men assigned to their respective shelters are currently being disciplined by action of the Conduct Adjustment Committee.

(signed)
R. Gohn
Deputy Warden

                    *   *   *

We turn now to the "Treatment" department. At the head of this department is a deputy warden, who is directly responsible to the warden for all prescribed policies and procedures relative to the individualized treatment of inmates: resocialization and rehabilitation. He also directs the supervisory heads of the following departments: Classification, Education, Vocational Training, Chaplains, Recreation, Music, Psychology, and Occupational Therapy.

The Classification Department

This department consists of a director, six full-time caseload counselors, and three part-time group counselors. The classification director functions as the supervisor of the counselors and as the coordinator of the Classification Committee which is responsible for all inmate work and shelter assignments. The Class Comm is made up of the directors of Education and Industry, along with the deputy wardens of Treatment and Custody; the committee meets twice weekly. Work and medical reports are obtained on all cases appearing before the committee; these, along with the remarks of supervisors releasing or requesting inmates, aid the committee to arrive at "objective" judgments. In the case of men appearing for Minimum Custody (trusty) consideration, the warden also interviews them.

In theory the classification program works well; in practice, however, it is a failure. Homosexuals, epileptics, the feebleminded, and the psychopaths are all lumped in with the general population. The young and the weak are mixed indiscriminately with the strong and case-hardened. Such muddling, though, cannot be avoided. The prison is overcrowded.

Men are different; and one of the aims of the Class Comm is to assign jobs and cells according to individual needs. Yet the smooth operation of the prison takes precedence over the needs of the individual. If a man is a butcher, and the Tag Shop needs more men, then the man goes there. It is hard to persuade a man who has been, say, a carpenter most of his life, and who is serving a 2-21 year sentence for killing a man in a fit of rage, that he is being "rehabilitated" when he is assigned to the mess hall to mop floors. By no stretch of the imagination can an assignment to the Tag Shop be considered rehabilitative; it is a job for which there is no demand whatsoever on the outside because all license plates throughout the country are made in the various state prisons. And, in the assigning of quarters, men are quartered in the "honor" dormitories not because of their individual needs, as such, but because of their good conduct—as a reward. Furthermore, men with long sentences are given priorities in jobs and cells simply because they have long sentences.

At present there are six counselors serving the entire prison population. Each counselor handles a caseload of approximately 350 men. He handles the mailing requests of those assigned to his caseload. He spends time at the information desk, assisting visiting friends and relatives of inmates. In case of domestic trouble, he tries to manage a workable relationship between the inmate and his family. He collects data on all new arrivals at the prison; he prepares "progress" reports for inmates appearing before the Parole Board. The counselor is in general a bridge between the inmate and the institution and the inmate and his family. Now, obviously, this large amount of work places definite limitations upon the quality of work done.

There are clearly not enough counselors; nor do those hired remain at the prison long. The work is too hard. The pay is too low. In his annual report to the warden, the present director of classification said: "The salary adjustments for counselors approved last year were expected to lower their turnover. And in spite of our continued personnel changes, there would undoubtedly have been more had it not been for these salary increases. Nonetheless, the starting rate of $450 per month for college graduates is ridiculously low. And this, coupled with annual increases of less than six dollars per week (when allowed!) makes retention of the *best* men impossible. Such a policy of salary administration guarantees retention of the *least* qualified personnel." [Emphasis and parenthetical remark in the original—E. K.]

Psychology Department

The prison maintains one full-time psychologist and one

part-time psychiatrist. (Because of the pay rate and the overwork, the turnover in psychologists is almost as rapid as with the counselors.) The work of the single psychologist is reduced to administering tests to new inmates and conducting psychiatric examinations, along with the psychiatrist, of those inmates whose behavior denotes mental illness. The chances are that an inmate with a mental illness will not be noticed as long as his actions do not upset the prison routine.

Education Department

The aim of the Education Department is to provide academic training to those inmates who are interested. The professional staff consists of six full-time teachers who are employed the year round and three part-time teachers who are employed during the summer months. Nine inmates serve as instructors in the elementary school and four as instructors in the high school. Both schools are fully accredited by the Indiana Board of Education, and the diplomas certifying completing of required courses are issued to graduates. College and trade school courses are also available to the inmates from the Indiana University Extension Correspondence and the International Correspondence. About 200 men attend school; the majority of them are in the elementary grades.

Recreation Department

Not ten years ago, in a prison in New Jersy, inmates had to pay their guards' salaries during evening yard time. Today, at the prison here some of the recreation equipment is paid for from the Inmate Recreation Fund, which consists of the profits from the prison commissary. That is to say, inmates are paying a higher price for commissary items in order to buy their own basketballs.

The recreation yard is approximately three football fields long and two football fields wide. In one corner of the yard is the gym, with a full-sized basketball floor and television sets ranged along one wall. Recreation periods are one night a week for each cellhouse and all day on weekends for all cellhouses. Inmates with spare time or off-duty are permitted on the yard during weekday mornings and afternoons. Recreation offers a variety of activities: baseball, basketball, boxing, football, tennis, weightlifting, wrestling, checkers, chess, and, along with many others, that favorite of all sports: TV watching.

In prison, recreation provides a very necessary outlet for pent-up emotions, and a majority of the men take advantage of the facilities.

Vocational Training

The various courses in vocational training are taught by twenty inmates and three civilians. Courses are offered in typewriter repair, refrigeration and air conditioning, carpentry, masonry, radio and television, auto mechanics, upholstering, and photolithography. In 1964-65, sixty-two men graduated from the classes; in 1965-66, forty-eight graduated. The curricula for the classes have been developed and approved by the Trade and Industrial Education Department of the State of Indiana. The institution itself provides a never ending source for project work and experience in typewriter repairing, radio and television, masonry and carpentry. The furniture used by the upholstering class comes from the state hospitals; materials and wrecked autos are donated to the mechanic's class by auto dealers.

All the courses in vocational training operate with little or no expenditures of state funds; most of the financial support is donated by various companies and organizations. Although the courses are devised and approved by the state, a man does not receive training from them comparable to vocational courses in the free world. There is no modern equipment; most of the televisions, radios, typewriters, autos, etc., are outdated. An effort is being made, however, to persuade large companies here in the state to send qualified instructors to the prison to train the men for possible jobs in the respective companies.

Religious Activities

Religious services for the men are provided by a Protestant chaplain, a Catholic chaplain and his assistant, and a Christian Science fieldworker. Jewish services are also held the first Saturday of each month by a rabbi from Michigan City. The chaplains also hold personal interviews, make hospital visits, and distribute religious literature. In his annual report to the warden, the deputy warden of treatment made the following recommendation for ". . . The construction of a completely new physical Chapel facility. The new facility should be a centrally located building of sufficient size as to be able to house all types of religious activities, regardless of denomination. Within this building would be separate offices of the Catholic and Protestant chaplains, a common sanctuary for worship services of all denominations, classrooms for Bible study and meditation. The use of this building would be restricted to religious activities and not serve as a multipurpose building as the present Chapel does for worship, movies, concerts, meetings, etc."

Parole Board

Ninety-five per cent of the sentences meted out by Indiana courts are indeterminate. Thus parole is the one thing uppermost in the minds of inmates.

Until 1967, the Indiana Parole Board was made up of three men, who held parole hearings once a month at the prison, the reformatory, the women's prison, the state penal farm, and at the institutions for boys and girls. This year there is a five-man parole board, the two men being added to it "in order to devote more time to each individual case." Over seven years ago, the *Chicago Tribune,* in an editorial, dated June 12, 1960, noted:

"At a recent one-day meeting at the Indiana State

prison at Michigan City, the Indiana Parole Board
interviewed 119 men. The board freed 29 on parole
and recommended 20 for discharge from parole. Parole
was denied to 18 applicants. Other decisions ranged
from "no change" to both parole and discharge. This
volume of work no doubt involved extensive preparation
by subordinates of the board. Even so, one would think
the parole board members must have felt uncomfortably
hurried. Some of the applicants, certainly, must have
felt that in so crowded a day their interviews were
disappointingly perfunctory. Unless the gentlemen on the
board are supermen, or unless it is all right for interviews with parole applicants to be so brief as to be
routine, the board settled entirely too much business
for one day's work. The public has a stake too, in the
parole process. Undue or misplaced severity adds to the
state's expense and makes it responsible for waste of
human life; undue or misplaced lenience denies society
protection to which it is entitled. Illinois, like Indiana,
has a part-time parole board. The citizens in each state
share both the cost of and the responsibility for any
mistakes arising from ill-considered parole board decisions."

A parole, logically, is the end, the icing for the rehabilitative cake. But is the parole system working?
From 1960 to 1965, 2,652 men were paroled; of that
number, 1,140 were returned as parole violators.

Parole boards are notoriously capricious. One man,
after being told by the board that he was being denied
a parole because of his past record, reasoned, "If they
set me for that this time, then they'll have to set me for
that from now on—cause my record will be the same
ten years from now." Another man, a Negro, as he was
being denied a parole, was asked accusingly by a
member of the board, "Why do you colored guys wear
those mustaches?" From then on, very few Negroes
appeared before the board with mustaches! A is told

that he is being denied because he has not taken advantage of the rehabilitation programs offered; B, who also did not participate in any programs, is granted a parole. These seemingly whimsical actions create a tremendous pressure on the inmates, causing some to abandon any attempts at self-improvement, causing others to become paranoid.

The unpredictability of the board, on the one hand, also creates trouble for a prison warden. Very seldom are his advice and recommendations heeded. And how does a warden explain the actions of a board to a man whose accomplice in crime, his "rap buddy," has been granted a parole when all available data on both men are the same. On the other hand, the parole board is a tremendous asset to the warden as a means of maintaining order in prison. Every inmate knows that in order to make a parole he must keep his "time clear." The queer reasoning seems to be that if a man can conform to the authoritarian routine of prison life, he will then be able to function positively in a free, competitive life on the outside.

Finally, when a man *is* paroled, he is given $15 in cash and a new suit of clothes (out of style) by the state. And most men leaving prison have nothing on which to rely until they can draw a paycheck. (During the years in prison he has earned an average of ten cents a day. A bar of soap costs twenty cents, in prison.)

Ninety-nine times out of a hundred, a man leaving prison is going to work on a blue-collar job, so the new suit of clothes is without utility. The fifteen dollars will hardly provide him with a place to stay—to say nothing of the personal necessities: work clothes, razor and toothbrush, etc. Because of all this, a man who has a wife or relatives on whom he must rely is from the outset put into an embarrassing, self-demeaning position. A man who has no wife or close relatives is forced to seek out old friends, usually those in an environment which quickly shoves him back into criminal activities.

Small wonder then that 75 per cent of all ex-convicts return to crime. Men are put into prison for the protection of society, it is said, but is it being protected when 90 per cent of all the men in prison will at one time or another be released and when 75 per cent of them return to crime?

Cell Song

Night Music Slanted
Light strike the cave
of sleep. I alone
tread the red circle
and twist the space
with speech.

Come now, etheridge, don't
be a savior; take
your words and scrape
the sky, shake rain

on the desert, sprinkle
salt on the tail
of a girl,

can there anything
good come out of
prison

The Warden Said to Me the Other Day

The warden said to me the other day
(innocently, I think), "Say, etheridge,
why come the black boys don't run off
like the white boys do?"
I lowered my jaw and scratched my head
and said (innocently, I think), "Well, suh,
I ain't for sure, but I reckon it's cause
we ain't got no wheres to run to."

A Brief History
of the Indiana State Prison

The Penal Code shall be founded on the principle of reformation, and not of vindictive justice. (Article 1, Section 18 of the Bill of Rights of the Indiana State Constitution.)

Before the first prison was established in Indiana, punishment for a crime was meted out at a public whipping post.

Thirty years before the Penal Code was enacted in 1851, the first prison was built in Jeffersonville, Indiana, at the cost of $3,000. It was made of logs and had fifteen cells in a row, with doors four inches thick and covered with strap iron. There was no light or ventilation except what came through an opening of about four inches at the top of the door. Rawhide whips were used on recalcitrant prisoners, and if that didn't keep them in line, there was always the dungeon.

Today, the cost of keeping just one man for one year at the Indiana State Prison is approximately $1,300. Today the cells at Michigan City have fluorescent lighting, steam heating, and transistorized ear radios. Solitary confinement has, recently, been abolished; prisoners are now punished by loss of privileges. And for honor prisoners there is *talk* of weekend "leaves." Much indeed has been added to better the lot of the convict, but as we trace the 156 years of the Indiana prison system we shall see if the "principle of reformation" has been followed.

The history of the Indiana penal system begins in vagueness and grew up in an air of political capriciousness. It seems that six years after Indiana was admitted to the Union, in 1816, the first prison was actually completed. It could hardly be considered more than a "stockade." In 1847, the "stockade" was replaced by the construction of a prison proper which was placed under the supervision of a warden. The prison, however, was overcrowded, and members of both sexes were allowed to mingle.

Public indignation soon started a movement for prisons of a correctional nature. But as is its nature, public indignation was short-lived, and nothing was actually done about the conditions in the Jeffersonville prison for a number of years. And the conditions grew progressively worse.

Then, in 1859, the State Legislature passed an act providing for the erection of a new prison, to be built north of the national road (U. S. Highway 40). The act granted $50,000 for the construction of the new prison on any 100-acre tract suitable for the purpose; it also appointed a Board of Control to select the prison site.

Enter politics.

On March 21, 1859, the Board of Control started its search for a favorable prison site. After it visited various Indiana towns, it finally chose Fort Wayne as the ideal site for the prison because, it is said, it believed that the prison could be built more cheaply there than at any other location.

Facts and recommendations were prepared by the Board of Control and sent to Governor Ashbel P. Willard for his approval. But for some reason Governor Willard neither approved nor disapproved of the location. So after a considerable length of time the Board of Control wrote to the Governor, informing him that they intended to buy the Fort Wayne site without his official sanction.

The purchase was never completed, however, because the state auditor refused to audit the account allotted to the Board of Control. The Board therefore reconsidered the location and decided upon the present Michigan City site.

Governor Willard immediately approved the location and signed the bill for its purchase; the state auditor was suddenly amenable; and, on March 4, 1860, the Board of Control purchased 100 acres of land from Chauncey B. Blair of Michigan City for $4,500.

The Governor then appointed Charles Seely, a member of the Board of Control, as warden. (The first warden was superintendent of construction, keeper, and general handyman. He was to have, for his own use, half of all the wood cut on the land and all the offal of the prison.) Warden Seely appointed Lot Day, Jr. as his deputy, B. D. Angell as clerk of the prison, and Dr. A. J. Mullen as physician. And the new prison was ready.

The first building used by the prisoners transferred from the old "stockade" at Jeffersonville was a hastily constructed wooden barracks surrounded by a board fence; and although the public was highly indignant over the conditions at the Jeffersonville prison, few changes were actually made in the new one. In the course of time and political maneuvering, however, public contracts were granted for the construction of more suitable buildings.

The plot thickens.

In January 1861, Warden Seely and Deputy Warden Day resigned, and Samuel Kirkpatrick of Tippecanoe County was appointed warden. But the 1861 legislature appointed a new Prison Control Board, and the newcomers promptly dismissed Kirkpatrick. Their nomination for the post of warden was Hiram Iddings.

At the same time, Richard Epperson of Montgomery County was appointed superintendent of convict labor. The first contract was granted to a Michigan City cooperage firm, whereby fifty convicts were contracted out for one year at thirty-eight cents a day. Business became so good through convict labor that the Governor decided to use more convict labor. More convict labor was used to build new industrial buildings; labor markets were actively sought out, and soon the prison was beginning to clear a little more than expenses. Convict labor had become big business.

The remainder of the century is clouded with wardens resigning, clerks absconding with prison funds, and general political confusion. Little, if anything, was done about prisoner rehabilitation.

The new century brought some little light to the prison darkness. In 1899, George Shideler became warden, and he quickly drew admiration from the prisoners because of his humanitarian methods. He threw out the whip and the cudgel, and in their stead used reasoning. He built a new officers' dining room and kitchen and enlarged the prison to twice its original size. But he was too "progressive" for the era in which he worked. Shouts of "coddling the convicts" were heard from certain quarters. And Warden Shideler left the prison in 1901 to become the superintendent of the Boys School at Plainfield, Indiana.

In 1907, the old Board of Control became the Board of Trustees. This four-man board acted as both the administrative body of the prison and the parole board until 1953.

The period from 1900 to 1967 is marked with innovations: a new commissary, new recreational facilities, and an accredited high school, to name a few. The physical plant of the prison has improved, by additions and alterations that abolished much of the former drabness in surroundings.

However, 52 per cent of the men released in 1965 on parole were returned to the prison as parole violators in 1966.

A WASP Woman Visits a
Black Junkie in Prison

After explanations and regulations, he
Walked warily in.
Black hair covered his chin, subscribing to
Villainous ideal.
"This can not be real," he thought, "this is a
Classical mistake;
This is a cake baked with embarrassing icing;
Somebody's got,
Likely as not, a big fat tongue in cheek!
What have I to do
With a prim blue and proper-blooded lady?
Christ in deed has risen
When a Junkie in prison visits with a Wasp woman.

"Hold your stupid face, man,
Learn a little grace, man; drop a notch the sacred shield.
She might have good reason,
Like: 'I was in prison and ye visited me not,' — or
  some such.
So sweep clear
Anachronistic fear, fight the fog,
And use no hot words."

After the seating
And the greeting, they fished for a denominator,
Common or uncommon;
And could only summon up the fact that both were
  human.

"Be at ease, man!
Try to please, man! — the lady is as lost as you:
'You got children, Ma'am?'" he said aloud

The thrust broke the damn, and their lines wiggled in
   the water.
She offered no pills
To cure his many ills, no compact sermons, but small
And funny talk:
"My baby began to walk . . . simply cannot keep his
   room clean. . . ."
Her chatter sparked no resurrection and truly
No shackles were shaken
But after she had taken her leave, he walked softly,
And for hours used no hot words.

Pages from a Prison Notebook

Sept. 1, 1963

Down the stairs from my cell five guys are laughing and horseplaying. They'll be silent and sad tonight after mail call if there is no mail for them — all but one cat. He calls himself "the tail-dragger," and he has the most distinctive laugh. You could easily identify it in the midst of ten thousand carousing convention-eers. He throws back his head, and his deep baritone rolls out of his throat like a well-oiled ball bearing, shaking and unsettling the air and bouncing and echo-ing over the tiers. Then it fades away, leaving an emptiness in the air, and in your chest.

Man is never as silly in private as he is in public.

The inmate-drivers who travel throughout the state delivering the products of the prison industries, shoes, soap, auto tags, and canned vegetables from the prison farm, are sometimes gone for two and three days. They got it knocked up.

Why are there always trains moaning their horns within earshot of prisons?

Each day enough bells are rung here to shatter the dreams of an opium-eater. No mail. Nothing happened unusual.

Sept. 2, 1963

There is a certain little fat foreman who I meet every morning as I come from breakfast and, rain or shine, hot or cold, he always has a bright "Good morning" on his lips. Now, mornings are a bad time for me. But lately I have noticed that after I have returned this little man's greeting, the fog clears somewhat. Perhaps he comes to work earlier than the other foremen because he is lonesome outside. I hear that he is a widower and childless.

I read that the seven most beautiful words in the English language are: Lure, Allure, Lilt, Flotilla, Downy, Moon, and Love.

Lester, twenty-two and indulgent, is getting in debt. In six months he'll be a faggot. Two poetry rejects. A letter from Momski. Statutory rape has been abolished in some states, while in others it has been made a misdemeanor, because everybody—even the politicians—knows that women, young and old, will falsify their ages. And other things too.

Sept. 3, 1963

The varsity weightlifting team will travel to Indianapolis tomorrow to compete in the all-city meet. I talked a great deal with Jim "No Toe" Wesby who heads the team and who holds ten state and national prison power-lift records. He is short and black and weighs 132 pounds. He got his nickname because he had to have a big toe amputated after it had been frostbitten as he hid from the police in a snow-covered field. I wouldn't doubt but that he tries to escape on his way to the city.

Got a letter from Dale tonight. She's salty cause Floydell's riding her back. She's probably nervous due to her pregnancy. Wrote Floydell a red-hot letter.

Sept. 4, 1963

"The credit belongs to the man who is actually in the arena. . . if he fails, at least he fails while daring

greatly, his place shall never be with those cold and timid souls who know neither victory nor defeat."
— Mahatma Gandhi.

Painted my cell today. Pastel blue. No mail, no rejects. "No Toe" didn't try to escape after all.

Sept. 5, 1963

First football game. Prison lost. Funny that all the guys should cheer for the outside team. Most of the Muslims got locked up today. The goon squad'll probably be after me next; I've been rapping with those cats a lot lately.

The following letter was written by G. D. to his counselor. He got fourteen days in the Hole for it.

Sir:

I am writing in a personal vein so that my concern regarding the parole board's directives may not be misunderstood. I am, of course, soberly aware of the mathematical duplicity inherent when one divides six counselors into two thousand men. That anyone could expect more than token results from such a formidable feat of algebraic gymnastics is, to my thinking, fatuous.

However, I am also conscious of this: should I choose to ignore the board's "suggestion" that I seek counselor help, not only would such a course be arrogant folly, but it would unquestionably result in my becoming a permanent resident in durance vile.

Do not, Sir, imagine that I write in a satirical frame of mind, nor that I am disdainful of counselor capabilities. Nothing could be further from the truth. It is one of my conceits that I am in tune with the times, and it is my feeling that counselors are necessary more than ever these days. They perform a yeoman service and under favorable conditions the results of their actions and functions can be extremely fruitful. In most respects I consider myself disgustingly normal with just a shade more than my share of character defects — the same type of defects that all humans this side of Olympus are endowed with. I am one of the "Karamazovs" that Dostoievsky so cleverly points out we all are. I believe a glance through my police folder (a dossier that has reached Homeric proportions) will reveal to even the dullest intellect the exact nature of my problem. Namely, that for twenty-six years I have been an uninhibited disciple of Bacchus.

And what to do about it? That, too, is clear and only I can do it. Acceptable insight or hindsight? I'm not sure. I wish, as did Burns, that "Would some power the giftie gie us/ to see ourselves as others see us." Lacking that gift, I stumble along like the rest of my species, sometimes profiting from the hard master, experience — and sometimes not.

Schiller wrote: "Mit der Dummheit kämpfen die Gotter selbst vergebens." Even in translation it has a certain pithy applicability, i.e., "With the stupid the Gods themselves battle in vain." Schiller, I suspect, came painfully close to the truth in my case. In any event, it would profoundly interest me to learn, with my narrow limitations, just how subtracting another year from a man's life will add to and improve his thinking.

To my thinking, that incredible theory upsets all the classical concepts of human behavior. Either the parole board is fifty years behind times or a thousand years ahead. To understand that type of *thinking* I most certainly *do* need help.

I look forward with lively interest to your opinions. When you have the time and the inclination, please summon G. D. to the Dark Tower come.

G. D. swears that the letter is his own creation, but I strongly suspect plagiarism. The letter has a familiar ring. But he has just got out of the Hole, and he does like to hurl big words around. He's a forger. Got a big-shot bag. Combs his hair over a bald spot.

Sept. 6, 1963

The most liked guard in the joint is J. P. He's a little gray-haired Pole who walks with a limp. Once he saved a con's life. A can of cleaning fluid, used between the Tag Shop ovens, exploded and showered the con with flaming gas. J. P. wrestled the panicky man to the floor and smothered the flames with his own body and hands. A second con died from burns suffered in the same accident. J. P. started working here in 1929. Says he's got nineteen grandchildren and is going to retire soon.

Janice's letters are getting longer and longer, and so is Momski's. Somebody should tell them that I can't act as referee in a maternal-filial bout. D. D. was brought back today on parole violation and a new charge. Nobody can make it on parole with a habit.

New curtains are being hung in the group therapy room. Ain't that nice. Getting to be more and more like home every day.

A wise man from Athens, when asked when injustice would be abolished, replied, "When those who are not wronged were as indignant as those who are."

Feb. 7, 1965

Sunday evening. My relaxing evening. Listening to jazz, disc-jockeyed by a soft-voiced woman. Wonder what Dale's baby is going to be like. Have got to do a thing about promiscuity and oppression.

The Whistler is on duty tonight. Somebody is bound to get busted.

Feb. 8, 1965

Death struck today. On the yard. This one gray cat sent his buddy, who had made parole, by his ol' lady's house, and his buddy copped righteous. Then his buddy came back on parole violation, and today they met on the Yard. And this cat busted the Lothario's head with a baseball bat. The blood from his head soaked into the sand around home plate.

Nothing but rejects. Lots of heat from the killing. Must be a bitch to die in prison.

March 13, 1965

Death penalty abolition vetoed today by Governor at the insistence of public. Public still demands human sacrifices. There are six men now on death row. One has been there for eight years. Death row and prison is but one sad chapter in a very sad book. A man should not be robbed and murdered in a dark alley; a man should not have his brain fried by 100,000 volts of electricity. Men should not have to spill their blood on battlefields, and little children should not have to go to bed with their bellies empty.

Might have to move back to C-Cellhouse. It is too noisy and distracting. Plus the Whistler's been eyeing my mustache and beard.

No mail.

He Sees Through Stone

He sees through stone
he has the secret
eyes this old black one
who under prison skies
sits pressed by the sun
against the western wall
his pipe between purple gums

the years fall
like overripe plums
bursting red flesh
on the dark earth

his time is not my time
but I have known him
in a time gone

he led me trembling cold
into the dark forest
taught me the secret rites
to take a woman
to be true to my brothers
to make my spear drink
the blood of my enemies

now black cats circle him
flash white teeth
snarl at the air
mashing green grass beneath
shining muscles
ears peeling his words
he smiles
he knows
the hunt the enemy
he has the secret eyes
he sees through stone

154

The Electric Chair

Last night they burned tough Tony
Who said he wasn't scared to die,
But with tears and screams Tony turned phony
When he kissed this ol' world goodbye.
— Traditional jailhouse poem

Indiana's electric chair has a gruesome distinction: the wooden part of it, the seat and the back, is made from the wood of a scaffold, on which Indiana hanged thirteen men before it adopted the Chair in 1914 as a more Christian and merciful way of killing. The Chair sits with a white sheet draped over it, like a covered shrine, in the rear of the deputy's office at the end of a long aisle that is lined on both sides by solitary-confinement cells.

Death row in the Indiana State Prison is situated on the ground floor of I-Cellhouse which is four tiers high, the top three tiers housing regular prisoners. In the afternoon, if the weather permits, the condemned men are let out, one by one, for an hour's exercise. A few of them spend a minute or two bouncing a basketball around but most of them simply pace up and down in the small wire-enclosed yard. Even though it's not allowed the regular prisoners often sneak down to the second floor and exchange a few words with the condemned men. And sometimes as I rap with one of them about the weather or the latest baseball scores, I wonder what is really going on in his mind.

I wonder if he realizes that he has become some kind

155

of sacrificial lamb, soon to be strapped onto a weird altar/throne so that the blood lust of a barbaric society will be quenched. I wonder if he knows that even if he does not die in the Chair he will still have served his purpose. Because when the newspaper headlines gloated: MAN SENTENCED TO DIE IN ELECTRIC CHAIR— That somewhere in the dark/bright regions of this society's mind it projected his death, walked the last mile with him, and licked its lips as he died in eye-bulging agony. So the question of capital punishment is merely rhetorical. It was never meant to deter crime, and the people who are pro-capital punishment on those grounds are hypocritical liars. No matter how sophisticated their argument, they are—in their souls—"eye-for-an-eye" fundamentalists. Because they, like everybody else, know that murders/homicides are committed under only two sets of circumstances: the man who kills deliberately and who doesn't think he's going to be caught, and the man who kills in a burst of passion/impulse without considering the consequences—and who wouldn't give a fuck about the consequences even if he did think about them.

But I never put any of these thoughts to the condemned men because they shy away from any serious conversation. They seem to know that their presence has cast an air of gloom over the cellhouse in the few weeks they have been here. Death row was previously on the second floor of the deputy's office, directly above the electric chair. It was moved so that the men could exercise and stay healthy. Like all sacrificial animals they must be kept sleek and healthy.

Besides the uniqueness of its electric chair, Indiana is like all the other man-killing states: it has electrocuted an unusually large number of black men. The youngest man sentenced to death in Indiana was black: sixteen. The youngest *two* men to actually die in the Chair were black: eighteen. The oldest man to die in the Chair was black: sixty-three years old. Out of twenty-four black men sentenced to death, only two received commutation to life imprisonment, while out of seventy-six whites, eleven received commutation. Only two black men out of twenty-four received new trials and a lesser sentence (life or two to twenty-one years), while fifteen whites out of seventy-six received new trials and lesser sentences. During one period however, 1935 to 1942, Indiana showed a deadly fairness by killing every man, black or white, sentenced to die. There are no available records as to the age or race of the men hanged by Indiana, but a rundown of the men sentenced to death in the Chair follows.

Number	Sentenced	Race	Age	Disposition
5565	10/22/13	W	40	Electrocuted 2/20/14
5571	10/30/13	W	35	Electrocuted 2/20/14
5806	6/16/14	B	34	Electrocuted 10/16/14
6089	3/22/15	W	27	New trial; acquitted
6183	5/22/15	B	23	Electrocuted 2/1/16
7833	7/ 3/19	W	23	New trial; life; paroled 10/1/43; discharged 1/22/44
7834	7/ 3/19	W	21	New trial; life; paroled 10/1/35; discharged 11/24/44
7835	7/ 3/19	W	21	New trial; life; paroled 10/1/40; discharged 11/7/43
7836	7/ 3/19	W	19	New trial; life; died on parole 6/17/29
8032	2/28/20	W	24	Commuted to life; paroled 2/28/45; discharged 8/7/59
8034	4/27/20	B	18	Electrocuted 8/5/20
8085	7/30/20	B	21	Electrocuted 12/10/20
8086	7/30/20	W	31	Commuted to life; paroled 8/7/40; discharged 11/21/47
8959	1/14/22	W	34	Electrocuted 12/1/22
8975	1/21/22	W	35	Electrocuted 6/1/22
9662	6/ 7/23	W	36	Electrocuted 11/14/24
10202	12/29/23	B	‑22	New trial; acquitted
10405	5/15/24	W	18	New trial; 25 years; paroled 5/15/36
10414	5/31/24	W	21	New trial; 25 years; paroled 5/21/34
10431	5/26/24	W	23	Commuted to life; died in prison hospital 7/28/29

Number	Sentenced	Race	Age	Disposition
10606	10/15/24	W	29	Electrocuted 1/30/25
11007	7/ 2/25	W	32	Electrocuted 10/16/25
11075	10/ 8/25	B	25	Electrocuted 1/16/26
11116	10/13/25	W	26	Electrocuted 1/22/26
11196	12/10/25	B	36	Electrocuted 3/26/26
11207	12/ 9/25	W	18	New trial; 2-21 years
11401	3/27/26	B	23	Electrocuted 3/26/26
11437	4/ 7/26	W	25	New trial; death; new trial; manslaughter, 2-21 years
11456	4/26/26	B	16	Commuted to life; paroled 2/22/50
11647	10/24/26	W	20	Electrocuted 4/10/28
13486	11/ 8/29	B	29	Electrocuted 7/1/32
13553	12/ 6/29	B	42	Electrocuted 3/21/30
13954	6/ 7/30	W	21	Commuted to life; paroled 9/18/45; discharged 1/11/60
14488	2/20/31	W	27	Commuted to life; paroled 12/28/49
14489	2/23/31	W	26	Electrocuted 6/24/31
14767	4/18/31	W	23	Commuted to life; paroled 3/19/45; discharged 1/28/60
14975	10/12/31	W	33	Electrocuted 2/12/32
15204	1/28/32	W	26	Electrocuted 11/24/33
15381	3/19/32	B	31	Electrocuted 10/1/34
15490	6/ 3/32	W	23	Electrocuted 7/28/33
15797	11/17/32	W	28	Electrocuted 3/2/33
15826	12/ 8/32	W	27	Electrocuted 9/28/34
16007	3/17/33	W	39	Electrocuted 3/2/34
16872	6/ 9/34	W	22	Electrocuted 10/9/34
17079	10/ 1/34	B	35	Electrocuted 4/17/36
17090	10/ 4/34	W	36	Commuted to life; died in prison hospital 6/25/51
17315	2/ 4/35	W	20	Electrocuted 10/19/35
17364	3/ 7/35	B	32	Electrocuted 6/14/35
18263	7/ 6/36	W	31	Electrocuted 10/19/36
18326	9/15/36	W	25	Electrocuted 12/26/36
18396	10/ 8/36	W	26	Electrocuted 9/17/37
18423	10/31/36	W	28	Electrocuted 1/14/38
18455	11/18/36	W	24	Electrocuted 3/12/37
18513	12/ 2/36	W	39	Electrocuted 5/6/38
18621	2/18/37	W	28	Electrocuted 6/10/37
18635	2/24/37	W	39	Electrocuted 6/10/37
18636	2/24/37	W	35	Electrocuted 6/10/37
18718	4/ 5/37	W	19	Electrocuted 7/8/38
18719	4/ 5/37	W	22	Electrocuted 7/8/38
19106	11/10/37	W	32	Electrocuted 9/30/38
19176	12/15/37	B	18	Electrocuted 6/23/39
19265	1/22/38	B	32	Electrocuted 5/3/38

Number	Sentenced	Race	Age	Disposition
19327	2/14/38	W	22	Electrocuted 6/1/38
19364	3/ 9/38	W	28	Electrocuted 6/28/38
---- (Federal prisoner)		W	32	Electrocuted 11/16/38
19619	8/31/38	W	25	Electrocuted 1/13/39
20041	5/ 6/39	W	31	Electrocuted 8/16/39
21160	12/24/40	W	24	Electrocuted 11/14/41
21622	10/21/41	W	33	Electrocuted 2/10/42
22365	5/24/43	W	43	New trial; life
22514	11/15/43	W	46	Commuted to life
23023	2/15/45	B	44	Electrocuted 4/2/46
23158	6/23/45	B	63	Electrocuted 11/26/45
23420	2/ 7/46	B	32	Commuted to life; died in prison hospital 8/2/51
23949	4/15/47	W	41	Commuted to life; paroled 5/16/68
24221	10/27/47	W	30	Commuted to life; transferred to mental hospital 2/23/66
24276	12/ 2/47	W	37	Electrocuted 2/23/49
24277	12/ 2/47	W	49	Electrocuted 2/23/49
24341	1/14/48	W	58	Electrocuted 3/29/49
24361	1/28/48	B	25	New trial; death; Electrocuted 1/16/51
25324	12/ 1/49	W	30	Electrocuted 12/30/50
26204	11/26/51	B	35	New trial; life
27431	11/28/54	B	27	New trial; life
28268	6/30/55	W	43	New trial; life
28603	1/ 9/56	W	31	New trial; life
29073	10/28/56	W	26	(Woman) Brought to institution, fingerprinted, then taken to women's prison. Sentence commuted one month later.
29421	5/24/57	W	37	New trial; death; Electrocuted 6/15/61
29687	11/ 1/57	W	53	New trial; life; died in prison hospital 11/9/61
29748	12/13/57	W	25	On Death Row
29833	1/ 9/58	W	58	New trial; life
30108	6/17/58	W	38	New trial; life
31052	4/21/60	B	27	On Death Row; new trial pending
31594	4/24/61	W	24	On Death Row
----	----	W	45	New trial; 2-21 years
32161	3/30/62	W	37	On Death Row
32500	11/ 5/62	W	55	On Death Row
32958	6/10/63	B	35	On Death Row
34299	10/12/65	W	28	On Death Row
34738	5/10/66	W	29	On Death Row
35582	12/11/67	W	24	On Death Row

To Make a Poem in Prison

It is hard
To make a poem in prison.
The air lends itself not
to the singer.
The seasons creep by unseen
And spark no fresh fires.

Soft words are rare, and drunk drunk
Against the clang of keys;
Wide eyes stare fat zeros
And plea only for pity.

Pity is not for the poet;
Yet poems must be primed.
Here is not even sadness for singing,
Not even a beautiful rage rage,
No birds are winging. The air
Is empty of laughter. And love?
Why, love has flown,
Love has gone to glitten.

The Day the Young Blacks Came

"We, the incarcerated black inmates at the Indiana State Reformatory, would like to have the following message printed in your newspaper at the earliest possible date. It is necessary that we draw the public's attention to the intimidation that the black inmates of this institution are receiving."

Thus began a letter in the "Letters to the Editor" sections of two Negro weeklies (The *Pittsburgh Courier* and the *Indianapolis Recorder*) during the second week of September, 1969.

The lengthy letter ran down a list of grievances ranging from "provincial-minded officials, officers as well as omnipotent administrators, who overtly express their vehement opposition to blacks," to specific instances of brutality, both psychological and physical:

"A few months ago, several blacks, namely, Lonney Gentry, Arthur Thomas, Gary Adams, and Melvin Johnson, were placed in isolation for reading literature written by black authors. While in isolation these men have been unsparingly harassed. On one occasion, they were sent a newspaper clipping (the clipping was sent to them by the official that unjustly placed them in isolation) describing the plight of a few Black Panthers held in Cuban work camps. Along with the newspaper clipping, these men were sent a note which asked, 'Do you still think Brother Castro is a black sympathizer? America is the best country in the world, fools.'"

161

After relating how "for no reason whatsoever" an inmate had been sprayed with chemical Mace so frequently that his skin had changed color, the black inmates told of the risk and possible repercussions confronting them for writing the letter. And then they closed with a plea: "We hope these words will fall on the ears of an empathizing society rather than an apathetic one. We plead for your assistance. . . ."

Evidently the plea of the black inmates went unheeded because a few weeks later, on September 27, 1969, the headlines of an Indianapolis daily newspaper blared:

REFORMATORY QUIET
AFTER RIOT KILLS 1
WOUNDS 46

The dead man was twenty years old, and the ages of the forty-six wounded ranged from the late teens to the early twenties. All of them were black.

According to the newspaper, some 400 inmates, the vast majority black, gathered on the recreation field and began shouting obscenities and hurling threats at the guards. After a short time the number greatly decreased, leaving only a determined group. Then, the guards, armed with riot guns loaded with bird and double-O shot, fired "over the heads of inmates and into the ground when about 100 prisoners threatened to burn down the institution and refused orders to disperse." Somehow, shotgun pellets "ricocheted off the concrete" and killed and wounded the black men. The news item further stated that the "disturbance apparently grew out of a [previous] disturbance . . . when seventy-five inmates staged a sitdown strike and demanded [that] their ten-point grievance be heard." A day before the riot occurred, six inmates had met with the prison superintendent "demanding the closing of the Hole, a solitary confinement cellblock, the releasing of four

Negro inmates who have been in the Hole since May
25, and an end to censorship of literature."

The item ended with a list of past "disturbances" inside the reformatory: In 1967, some sixty inmates set
fire to the reformatory mess hall; during that same
year, twenty-five prisoners captured a guard, locked
him in a cell, and then shattered windows and burned
mattresses; two inmates were also killed in 1967, "allegedly by fellow prisoners." In 1968, a counselor was
beaten; an inmate was knifed; in another incident, guards
had to fire "three shots into the air" to disperse a group
of prisoners. Finally, in August, 1968, a group of
"inmates were transferred to the Indiana State Prison
at Michigan City after a demonstration over food service
and alleged racial discrimination."

The young man, shot in the head, crumbling to the
ground, the still smoldering buildings, fired by the en-
raged prisoners; the bloodsplattered recreation field
where forty-six men lay wounded, is just one tragic scene
in a drama that began with the above-mentioned group
of young black men who were transferred to the Indiana
State Prison some thirteen months ago. Would the recent
riot have occurred if those men (some of whom were
involved in both "disturbances") had been listened to,
looked at? Is the drama over now that blood has been
drawn or is the real climax yet to come? What kind of
young men are these who, naively hoping that their
pleas will be heard, write long, impassioned letters
to a historically apathetic society? What do they think
and feel?

Perhaps some of these questions will be answered in
the letters presented below, letters that were written,
some by me and some by three of the transferred men,
after they came to the State Prison and while they were
still locked up on "the Rock" — a maximum isolation
facility, the prison within the prison. The letters are
presented here exactly as they were written. The writers

had no idea that their words would be read by anybody but me; they were simply expressing themselves
to a brother. Because the letter writers are still in prison,
I have not used their true names.

But first, a few words about the day the young blacks
came and how they shook up the joint with their blackness and their boldness.

The morning of August 5, 1968, began like all other
mornings in prison: dismally. A thick fog, rising out
of nearby Lake Michigan during the night, had crept
over the walls and permeated the prison, perfectly match-
ing the miasma in our minds. By midmorning, however, the sun had swept the fog away. And we had settled into our usual routine when the news of the arrival
of "some young brothers from downstate" rumbled
through the prison like an earthquake, shaking us out
of our lethargy. Within minutes a crowd of onlookers
lined the street leading to the admissions building.

Through the back gate in the south wall the young
ones came. Chained and manacled like a coffle of slaves,
they hobbled along in their leg irons. They wore their
hair long, flaring out from their heads, and *tikis* and
other charms hung around their necks. And as the
line hobbled along, the young men would raise their
manacled hands in the Black Power sign as they smiled
or shouted to some recognized onlooker.

The guards, of course, soon broke up the crowd.
As we moved away, one old black man said, "Them
young fools are in for a whole lot of trouble. Somebody
oughtta talk to them niggers so's they don't make it
hard for all of us." Another man replied, "What are you
talking about, muthafucka? It can't get no worse. I'm
glad they're here 'cause them young niggers just ain't
gonna take the shit that we took off the white man."

At noon the mess hall buzzed with conversations
about the new arrivals. And despite the fears and anx-
ieties expressed by some of the older black convicts

in regard to the militant posture of the young blacks, there was a general air of pride among the black population — an almost imperceptible lifting of the shoulders. (In the months to come, the beneficial effect of the young blacks on the older ones was to be proved: knifings and fist-fights among "brothers" decreased; the boxing program, once a main sports interest, went out of existence; interest in things "black" increased to such a degree that a history book, such as Lerone Bennett's *Before the Mayflower*, was worth ten cartons of cigarettes — prison currency; and even though the guards tried to break them up, gangs were formed to protect the more timid young blacks from some of the old convicts who wanted to make "girls" out of them.)

After the noon meal I made the rounds of the cellhouses, gathering books, and at suppertime I sent them up to the Rock by the trusty who takes the food to the men in isolation. The next week the trusty brought me a letter and said, "The dudes want you to smuggle it out." The letter, written on prison stationery, was addressed to a person in the Justice Department. I smuggled it out:

August 16, 1968

Civil Rights Division
Washington, D. C. 20530

Dear Sir:
This letter, I assure you, if completely disregarded, may be detrimental to fifty-five persons who were involved in the situation I will explain to you.

I am presently an inmate at the Indiana State Prison. On August 4, 1968, I and fifty-four other inmates of the Indiana State Reformatory at Pendleton, Indiana, were abruptly transferred to the State Prison here as a result of a peaceful sit-down demonstration protesting conditions and the racism which was being practiced by the institutional court as well as many, or almost all, of the officers of the Reformatory. Our action followed the presentation of a list of grievances to Mr. Anthony S. Kuharich, Commissioner of the Indiana Department of Corrections. (All previous attempts to acquire results through "the chain of command" had proven futile.)

Our main objective was to persuade Mr. Kuharich to present himself to us and explain why those situations and conditions existed and why he couldn't make changes that were definitely necessary. He directed Mr. Valjean Dickinson, Asst. Commissioner, to talk to us. Why Mr. Kuharich refused to present himself to us remains a mystery. But all this is immaterial to the problem we are now confronted with.

However, I think I should mention that Mr. Dickinson explained to us that direct orders were, or had been, given by Mr. Kuharich, to disperse us verbally, and if necessary — by any means, regardless of the results. When we requested again for Mr. Kuharich to present himself to us, helmeted officers armed with shotguns surrounded our group. Again we were informed of Mr. Kuharich's orders and told that we had a choice: either to disperse and return to our respective cellhouses (upon entering cellhouses, names and numbers were to be given to cellhouse officers — an indication that solitary confinement was surely to follow), or we could "volunteer to be transferred to the State Prison." Naturally, sensing the inhumane treatment that would have taken place if we had dispersed, we all *volunteered* to be transferred to the State Prison.

Upon our arrival here we were informed that our actions at the Reformatory were in the past and the officials were concerned only with how we conducted ourselves at this institution. But we were immediately incarcerated in an "isolation" section of the prison and were given the excuse that due to the large number of inmates, job assignments would take some time. Actually, this was to be the first of our punishments.

And so our ordeal began. Confined twenty-four hours a day with only a fifteen-minute period once a week — sometimes once every two weeks — for showering and shaving. We were constantly being provoked to cause some sort of disturbance so that the officers could, willingly, exercise the use of chemical Mace.

All fifty-five of us tolerated every provocation; we endured until human endurance reached its limit. We were punished for even asking why we were absolutely forbidden to talk to each other. (On arrival here we had been given a pamphlet of rules and regulations for the "isolation" section, and one of the rules was that talking was permitted but was to be held at a minimum.) Regardless of our efforts to obtain an explanation, we were tear-gassed in the cells. Already behind bars, securely locked in, and still we were tear-gassed. It became a regular action. Some fellow inmates have even been tear-gassed from behind. (Through air vents on the back wall of each cell.)

At one time, on the midnight shift, an officer was walking past our cells, taking a head count. By his motions when walking, he seemed to have been intoxicated. When a few inmates questioned the officer, he walked away and returned with pencil and pad and began taking cell numbers at random. Everyone was unaware of what he was doing. But we found out the following morning when we learned that *nineteen* of us had been booked (institutional arrest). I will not relate the details of the kangaroo trial; only that some of us — almost all of us — were found guilty and sentenced to "seclusion" in the Deputy's office (another form of solitary confinement). At one period some of us were in total darkness for as long as twenty-four hours. And I understand it is against the law for any institution to totally isolate an inmate.

However, our main concerns now are the inmates

who are still in "isolation" and the orders handed down by Mr. Kuharich, instructing the Indiana Parole Board to take further action for yet additional punishment.

Two of the fifty-five inmates have already made appearances before the parole board. Both were questioned about the incident that occurred at Pendleton, and both were given an additional year. And it is the opinion of persons such as the Catholic chaplain here that the same thing will happen to all of us. Is there anything you can do to aid us? Many of the men were indeed deserving of a parole, and probably would have received one, had the incident not occurred on August 4.

Sir, I stress the fact that on August 4, 1968, not one bit of violent action was taken by any of us. When the riot-helmeted and armed officers surrounded us, we remained seated on the ground to wait for an explanation from someone. We uttered not one word of violence. (How could we even breathe with fifteen to twenty shotguns pointed directly at us?) We had no weapons — although a few of us were armed with Bibles and Coca Colas.

What is most pressing is the punishment being inflicted on the men who are still in "isolation."

I would also like to stress that Mr. Kuharich was clearly aware of the situation before, and on, August 4, as he had refused to present himself to discuss our grievances. He is also aware of our predicament here. Sir, we had not asked for color televisions or steaks every day, or for conjugal visits. All we requested was improvement of kitchen and eating facilities and a more equal treatment of all inmates regardless of race, color, or religion.

I also wish to add that a number of inmates have been retransferred back to the Reformatory at Pendleton for various reasons, but the main reason is to escape the inhumane treatment received since our arrival here.

This inhumane treatment and the additional year

meted out by the parole board are uppermost in our minds.

All I ask for, and I speak for us fifty-five victims of a seventy-five years old correctional system, is some form of Justice, as our most precious asset is at stake. . . our freedom.

I remain . . .

Respectfully yours,
[I have omitted the name and number of the prisoner who signed this letter. — E. K.]

After I had smuggled out the letter to the Justice Department I "flew a kite" to the Rock informing the men. That same day the trusty brought me a letter from "Slim," thus beginning an exchange of "kites" that lasted for some twelve weeks. (Realizing that in some of the letters the men, including myself, were simply killing time, "shucking and jiving," I have deliberately chosen the most argumentative, hoping that in them the men's truest feelings will be revealed.)

* * *

August 18, 1968

Dear Brother Knight,

I am wondering whether you have taken care of that business yet. Because its important that something be did about this mad dog concentration camp. I have done a lot of reading lately and things are really beginning to fall in line. Although you didn't send any books directly to me, but I got possession of a few and have been sending word out to you to look out for me, since I can't look out for myself, as far as getting

books. Look Knight, to be honest, I am shitty at you
and the rest of these so call black brothers who know
that I haven't did a dam thing to get lock up, but
yet and still they so fucking afraid of this punk ass
honky until they just stand back and see a brother
getting frame up and being victimized without opening
up their mouth in attempt to stop these mad dog honkies
from fucking over black people. The thing I think they
don't realize is that the same way I am a victim of
nothing, they too are going to be victims of the same
thing, nothing, no more than them being black. We
really need some kind of unity and brotherhood, and
the only way I can see us getting this in this racist
institution is through a black history class. These black
brothers are not aware of what really is going on,
because if they were aware, they wouldn't be setting
down, keeping cool, being victimized and all the rest
of that so call honky humane bull shit. You don't act
refined when some motherfucker is trying to kick you
in the ass or take your life, you forget about refineness
then. But I'll suffer like I have suffered before from
my confinement for nothing in hope that I will some
day have the privilege to throw the last brick. I wish
you luck in front of the [Parole] Board when you go.
                                                              Slim

                                                      9/12/68
Hey Slim —
    Peace. Are you still shitty? That brother brought me
a *Liberator*, but it's an old one. Don't you receive them
anymore? Dig, if you have read the latest *Ebony* I
want your opinion of the article by Llorens. If you don't
have it, let me know and I'll see that you get it next
week. When you finish with it send it on to Water, I
want to see what he thinks of the article, too. Ain't
nothing going on out here, man. The same old bull-

shit. We're all uptight. Hold on, Baraka. Next year will be the year of Liberation.

Peace,
Knight

9/12/68

Say Guy,

I'm beginning to wonder just how far submerged are you in this white wash. This is the second time you have mentioned something about them low lifed hunky politicians doing us a favor. First it was _____ and now it is _____, and it used to be you that would try to tell me something about the nature of the enemy. The only thing that one of those swines has ever done for anyone is something that enhance their position. Over 300 years ago the Indian recognized him as the most notorious liar on the face of the earth and labeled him, forked tongue. (And today you are talking about one of them hunkies owing you a favor. Unbelievable!!) You seem to be going in a different direction from the rest of the blacks here. Oh yes! Mama even told me don't trust any of them when she was up here and I was telling her about that hunky Commissioner I'm locked up for. And if you don't mind me saying that is quite a feat for her not to trust any of them. So don't ever tell me anything about what one of them hunky dogs doing somebody a favor. It is beginning to appear that you're a very gullible, unaware, potential Uncle Tom. Maybe if you would stop thinking the only thing that a nigger has to do in order to be black is to avow to hate whitey, look extremely hard, and never smile, you can wake up to the nature of the enemy. I would like to point out something to you (Tom), I hope you don't think that I'm mad at you because I'm not, but it is getting sickening for these so called evangelists of blackness talking about their hunky friends, their trust in the swines will end up with some of my people tricked write into a gas chamber. Bucky has my book, *Black Power*. Just send up here for it, because you definitely need to read it. I really enjoy them black newspapers, they really something. Why don't you see if Sonia will send me the picture of a black girl student wearing a natural. I think that they are really beautiful. I realize that you're not a subscription department but send some more books.

Water

9/12/68

Water—

Peace. Look, I am going to ignore all of your wild rhetoric for the moment, but I have to say this: who in the fuck are you to rave and rant and call anybody an Uncle Tom when you are supposed to have so much love for yourself, your family, and for black people, and yet you blow your chance to go home where you can really do something—all because you can't keep your mouth shut up there. Even a Tom wouldn't do that, so before you take the role of criticizing somebody you get your own ass together. A man is not what he says, but what he does. Now that I got that off my chest, Peace. Dig, I'll hit on Sonia about that natural-haired sister, okay? Hold tight.

Peace,
Knight

9/16/68

Brother Knight,

First of all I would like to tell you that you're not such a brilliant minded person or such a hypersensitive delicate thing that you're above criticism. Whenever I feel that your action is showing defects I will say so.

My main concern now is where are we going as a people and in what role am I going to play. I really would like to be a black panther when ever I get out of prison. Since I did my in depth study of our problem in this country, I could easily kill any hunky in the world if it would aid in freedom. Some book that I read said that the hardest thing to shake is the conditioning that you're doing something wrong if you destroy the slave master. I have no love what-so-ever for my enemies black or white. All whites aren't my enemies but the system and the bigots are. I'm sending you *Dark Ghetto*, send it back. Also send me those articles by Cleaver. There's no hurry.

Water

The most profuse of the letter writers was Bucky, a twenty-two-year-old poet and one of the "leaders" of the group. Our exchange of letters was, from the outset, hot and heavy. In my first letter to him, I criticized the "demonstration" that he had led at the reformatory, saying that it was immaturely staged, that he was naive and misleading the men by believing that some "outside" help would be forthcoming. He replied:

9/27/68

Brother Knight,

I agree that we should not expect people to help us. Now, when I say people I mean primarily ofays and toms. I also realize that the brothers on the streets, who would help, have their hands full, therefore we should not expect too much out of them. However, this still does not give us the right to lay down here. I know you feel that one should wait until he has a certain amount of free movement, but I want to ask you this, Knight: is there a battle to be won here? I also ask: is this battle here a part of the war? If your answer happens to turn out yes, then I will ask: who is

more able than us to understand the situation, fight it
accordingly, stamp it out, thereby rendering our duty
to the cause and make the brothers' work lighter in
the street? The truth is that you only want to be success-
ful as a writer and poet. Say man, I'm hip to your
thing. You don't want to blow here because you don't
think the situation deserves you. Not with all the ability
you have. I know you say: why should I waste myself here when I can go to the streets and do so much
more. Now ain't that how it is, baby? It's just that I
differ a wee-bit with you inasmuch as I will fight
wherever the battle is, here, on the streets, or in hell.
I just happened to pick up the prison paper and saw
your poem under the heading: "Lend Me Your Ear"
and I thought: Why, this tomming ass nigger ask for
someone's ear outside the prison walls and there is a
war going on under his nose. Well, you know how
nuts write to columnists and shit talking about them and
saying absurd stuff? Well, I just happen to be one of
those guys. You should have read the letter and forgot
the thing. But by me being black, you didn't want me to
have a tommish concept of you. I was merely expressing
why I couldn't lend you my motherfucking ear. I know
you are now saying, "Look nigger, I have tried to be
nice to you, I have even made special efforts." But you
see, Knight, a man's actions speak for him. You've been
here five years and couldn't even get a black history
class started. So don't tell me nothing about waiting.
When you die, they should put on your tombstone,
He Waited. You told me that our thing at Pendleton
was immature, misdirected, etc. What I would like for
you to do, Mr. Knight, is show us how to do it right.
We are more than willing to learn. Man, you know, I
really dig these guys up here on the Rock. Their spirits
are riding high and what's so beautiful is that there
is no sign of them coming down. Man, these guys (fifteen
and up) layed me out down to Pendleton. When those

hunkies ran out with the shotguns and said, "Move or we are going to shoot," my knees turned to water, but you know what those fifteen-year-old guys said to them: "Shoot hunky, you ain't said nothing." I have never heard anything like that in my *life*. And don't you think that they didn't mean it. Being a part of that was like receiving ten years of college. What an experience. I have a hard time trying to direct all this energy up here. What they want to do is do the thing *again*. Hey, and by the way, Malcolm was not an honor prisoner, he was moved because his sister Ella pulled a few strings, remember? Brother, you don't know how bad I want to go home too. I got a woman out there who loves me and a Mom who I love. But I love the black people and mankind more than I do them as individuals. I must fight the enemy wherever I confront him, because I am a *MAN*, and I wish you'd become one, too. I see you have taken the time to lecture me on points of culture. I am going to make this short. Culture, I understand in its essence: its forms, the norms, group expectations and its institutions. Brother I know the thing inside-out and outside-in. I also know that we are enslaved. And culture ain't never freed nobody, only guns have done that. Dig, I am sending you some poems. Type them up and see if you can send them out. Will close for now. I hope you get yourself together.

Bucky

Within a few days I had the poems typed up and ready to be sent on their way to the outside. I sent carbon copies of them to Bucky, along with the following letter:

10/6/68

Brother Bucky —
Peace. First, the poems. As you can see, I have put

your name to them. They are good poems — very good. But back to your name: dig, I'm hip to that anonymous shit. You're the kind of dude my daddy used to talk about — one who "throws a rock and hides his hand." No good. You got to take responsibility for your words, for what you say and what you write. If you're going to presume to speak to black people as a black poet, then you are held responsible to the people. Under the cloak of anonymity you can be as irresponsible as you want to, can't you? No good, baby. I can hear you saying that the "cause" is the only thing that matters, and that *sounds* good and is true but meaningless in this particular case.

LECTURE: No matter how bad your handwriting is, when submitting a poem, the poet should make sure that the poem is finished, is free from errors and is *legible*. The poet who submits sloppy work shows that he has no respect for the poem or for the reader, that is, for black people. END OF LECTURE.

Still, brother, if you won't come out of that anonymous bag, I will send them out like that. I just wanted you to know that I see through that jive, and I hope you will reconsider and be man enough to stand behind your words. Now that I've gotten that off my chest, we can move on to other things. Incidentally, there are poems of mine that have been printed that I now wish I hadn't written. I mean, I would like to say that I have always written, and thought, black, but that would be ignoring history, denying it. Like almost everybody else, I was in the integration bag. And so were you, big bad wolf. (I guess you know that the lecturing tone of my words are the privilege of age — not necessarily of wisdom. A habit that is hard to break.)

You will find enclosed a couple of Sonia's poems. I would like to know what you think of them. She is having a small book published this spring. I'll see that you get a copy. Dig, ask Slim if he received my kite. Also, very reliable sources say that Snooky has a gray chick. What do you say to that?

Now look, brother, this hangup you got about being a man, or rather, about us being men, I'll go through just one more time with you. Dig, I agree that manhood, in most cases, comes out of direct confrontation with the enemy. What you obviously do not know is that I went through my baptism of fire a few years ago. I went through it, baby, when it was *really* dangerous. We didn't have the protection of being "young," we didn't have the protection of this sham atmosphere of genteel liberality. They sent troublemakers to the nuthouse, and burnt their heads to a crisp with shock treatments; they had *HOLES*, not nice cells with mattresses and radios and cigarettes and books. So you don't have to run your man thing down to me. I been there. And it ain't no big deal, not big enough — at any rate — to give you license to preach and berate any and everybody who does not happen to see the sky in exactly your shade of blue.

Peace. Hold on — more pleasant things coming up. I think I know what you mean about those young brothers. They are indeed beautiful and to have been with them must have been a wonderful experience for you. I think it would have been for me too. And I did not mean to de-emphasize the importance of what went down. What I'm saying, brother, is: be careful that you do not become messianic because of that experience. True, I guess we all are, or must become, a little messianic, if we are to survive all this ofay bullshit that is bombarding our brains. But we must always leave the doors of our minds slightly open.

You asked me once if it is possible not to love one's self. Yes, if one has no sense of, no concept of self, in a positive sense, then he could not possibly love himself, now could he? And it is true that understanding

is one of the things that moves one toward freedom.
But again, before one can understand his situation, the
nature of his existence under oppression, he must first
understand that he exists. Understanding stems from
love, is in fact a component of love. This awareness
of "the masses" that Fanon and the Marxists speak of
does not quite fit our situation. Do you remember Malcolm telling about this house nigger that identified with
the slavemaster to such an extent that when the slave-
master's house caught on fire, the slave said, "Massa,
our house is on fire." Do you think that slave had any
awareness of himself or his situation?

The African, even under colonialism, maintained a
kind of identity through the indigenous culture. The
structures of tribalism always told him exactly who he
was. But our situation is different, and to say otherwise
is stupid. And if you know the cultural thing inside-
out, then you know that we are literally creating a
nation and that cultural structures are as important
as economical and political structures. *Without cultural
structures we will not know which way to go.* And
since culture is dynamic/living it will be a revolutionary
culture if *we* are revolutionary. Even you admit in your
poem, "Big Red," that we ain't agreed on the right
road to freedom. Got to go for now.

Peace,
Knight

10/10/68

Big Brother,

You know, you lay me out. You tell me you have the
right to lecture or the privilege to lecture by virtue of
your age and experience. That really makes me want
to get off into a thing, but fuck it. As far as using my
name to the poems, go ahead. Knight, this may sound
terribly silly to you, but dig this: about my style, being

"free from errors," etc. — and, oh yes — "sloppy," now, to me, all this style and correctness shit don't mean a damn thing. Conventions, traditions, don't interest me; in fact here is where the mind is bound by the slave-master. There is a revolution going on and I shall adhere true to the principle, *complete* change. So anyway you see my jive, whether it be sloppy, shitty, foul, ir-rational, stupid, sane, correct, or *anything* you can name, that is the manner in which I express myself and the pulse of my involvement. So what you see in my stuff is *me*. I am now close to breaking all of my prior conditioning and have tried as much as possible to not use the slavemaster's language.

Sure, I have been in that integration bag in the truest tommish sense. I too have poems that are not fit for the cause, but I keep them to remind me of the stages of my development. Hey, they are transferring some of the guys back to Pendleton. Brother, this is the first Hole I have been in that has had a mattress. Two weeks before our thing went off down at Pendleton, I spent twenty-two days on *concrete*, half rations and a cup of water a day. I had to tom my way out by promising to give up the teaching of my history and remain silent. Now, before that, I had just did six months on A&S (like the Rock here), and before that, Hole, Hole, Hole. . . . Ask Chan or some of the other guys. Hey, I am having a thousand and one problems with these guys up here. I went through a thing last night that really made me sick. I wanted to express the point to them that there is more to it that hollowing Honky, Honky, Honky, Honky. We had a real thing and I blew my cool. I am very shitty at the dudes and myself. These guys seem to think they can make the honky afraid by calling him names. You know, this has been going on now for quite a few nights, so I tell the guys, "Man, everything we say or do, the hunky knows it. When he receives his report on us it says we are talking about killing him, we will never get off this Rock." I said, "There is nothing wrong with the plays but we must consider our situation." [The plays were out of the Black Arts Theater.] And dig what kind of response I get from the guys: "Ain't nobody scared of the honky, fuck him!" You know, shit like that. I wanted to give up the ship. Man, I can not stand ignorance, one of the reasons I fight so hard to get it out of me. Contrary to what you believe, I don't assume the role of a leader, it's just that if a motherfucker is laying behind I will run way out in front. But not because I want to be out front, I am chasing the cause, man, and I want to catch up with it. You asked once if I have ever been wrong about anything. No, essentially, for the last five years I have not! Black Power is on its way. Don't panic! I only mean the book. Ha! Curly Bill will bring it to you. Hey, I just heard that there was a riot at Pendleton. Spells trouble. That Kuharich is trying to suppress the news. The guy wants to save his job and is *dangerous*. Hey man, whitey is reading our kites. *Don't run for the wall!* Ha! Ha! Ha! I know by now you are shittier than a motherfucker. Just thought of something, since you have tremendous trouble hearing me, hear Fanon: "The colonised man who writes for his people ought to use the past with the intention of opening the future, as an invitation to action and a basis for hope. But to ensure that hope and to give it form, he must take part in action and throw himself *body* and soul into the national struggle." I just underline the body for you. Hey man, ha, I am cutting out. The guy hasn't brought the books up yet. Hope I get to see you before you split on parole.

Bucky

10/12/68

Dear Bucky —
    Just got your kite this a.m. The dude laid it on me

while I was still in bed (was up late last night writing
a poem to you brothers) and after reading your kite
I lay there and laughed my ass off. You're something
else. First, let me say this: Brother, I was not criticizing
your poetry, I was criticizing the *submission* of it. If
your poems are going to be read, any fool knows they
must be legible. All I meant was how will the reader
know you meant t-h-o-t if the letters look like #$%&?
I agree that most traditional shit ain't shit, but how
is one going to know how to get away from traditional
shit if he doesn't know what traditional shit is? Hell,
free-form verse ain't new, or European. African and
Oriental artists were blowing free hundreds of years
before Rimbaud, Verlaine, and others like that. But
enough of this. Here are some specific questions that
I would like to have your honest opinion on: What
do you mean by "complete change?" What is your
conception of nationalism? How exactly do you see
Black people achieving freedom? And don't just say
by fighting—give me a general picture. Did you read
David Llorens' article in *Ebony* on separatism? What's
your reaction to it? Also, have you read the latest
Journal of Black Poetry? Be cool, and tell the guys
to hang loose.

Peace,
Knight

10/16/68

Brother Knight,
   It is very difficult to describe our (black folk) life
using whitey's words and forms. As for you criticizing
my work, hey, do your thing. I wish I could get you
to understand though that I don't value critics at all,
and opinions less than that. Dig it? The little poems
I write I value them only inasmuch as they are able
to shed a little more light on the situation. I don't in-
tend to get a hole in my soul by trying to be a "suc-

cessful" writer. But I think you want to be accepted by
the general public, and brother, that's W-H-I-T-E. The
revolution is B-L-A-C-K. Dig that? One of those Negro
guards down at Pendleton called me a fascist and reac-
tionist, and I told him that he was right, that I would
react everytime. Say, I received the last shipment of
books you sent. Hey, this *Ten Black Writers Respond*
ain't shit, in fact it's less than that. All those niggers
are toms. I read the introduction and that's all. These
niggers are shitty because this hunky has made a pile
of money off of his book. The thing that fucks me up
is this: Why in the hell didn't these niggers write the
accounts of Nat Turner? They were too goddamn busy
writing about the white man and trying to show whitey
that contrary to what has been said, there are some
good and intelligent Negroes. There should be at least
twenty books about the excellent thing Nat did. But
until lately all the niggers have been ashamed of Nat's
conduct. Dig that? I am not going to pollute my mind
by reading it. It's bullshit. Dig this: Toms (and most
black writers are toms) are made not born. In the instances where I have referred to you as being a little
tommish is because I'm at the point where I count only
achievements. And you don't have many on the books.
You can't tell me that you couldn't (in five years) establish some type of work shop for the guys here. It
doesn't make sense. If you know these guys were lacking in readiness then why didn't you prepare them.
You spoke once of *fear*, why didn't you try to remove
some of it from among the brothers? If you are aware
that physical force is stupid under these conditions, why
didn't you institute another method? I have never felt
that I have a divine mission, but I do know that I have
a duty. Now, I see here where you want to see my thing,
dig it: When I say complete change, I mean a complete
changing of this system which will be brought about
by those who are aware. And brother, I am going to

be among that number. Now, what we are going to change to is not as important as getting this load off of our backs as soon as possible. In changing the present situation we ourselves will certainly change, we will develop something new. But let me go on a little. I have been asked this same question by many people, what are we going to change to. My response it, let events take their course. But you are looking, for a map to show you the way. Life doesn't develop like that. To say that if we can't think of anything immediately better than this, why not hold this until such a time as we do come up with something? Those who hold this idea are ignorant. With the lion eating your ass now, why worry about the bear in the woods? At least you have never been bitten by the bear. Dig it? But you already know how the lion is, he ain't cool. The whole thing boils down to this: We, the aware, must make as many among the masses as possible to understand our plight. But it's not necessary that the entire mass be aware; let those who are aware be capable of moving the mass in the desired direction. Now, the thing about nationalism. As you know, nationalism contains a number of things, the major ones being common values, speech, habits, beliefs, and a generally agreed upon type of government. Therefore, in order for us blacks to embrace nationalism we must also embrace Americanism unless we change our value system which has been a white one. Maybe that's what this culture shit is all about. Now, you take me. I'm against this system, but I still like Cadillacs. I got to cut this short. Want to catch the dude when he brings up the food. You know, man, I had a beautiful surprise today. My family came down and both of my sisters wore Afros. I never thought those two would wake up. Just goes to show you there are things to wake up the dead. I wonder what's wrong with some people? Take care.

Bucky

A Time to Mourn

He stepped out of the darkness and hypnotic noise of the prison tag shop into a sea of sunshine spilling like foam-tipped waves off the high slaty-gray walls and washing the asphalt street and Industry Buildings in sheets of heat. He pulled his cap down over his eyes and followed the deputy warden's messenger across the street and down a spotless sidewalk that cut a surgical path through the neatly mowed lawn, which lay like a green carpet crisscrossed by white walks and dotted with great circular beds of flowers and whirring lawn sprinklers. He heard lazy shouts floating in the oppressive air and the sharp smack of a baseball being slammed; to his left, he saw a few men shagging flies out on the baseball field whose bare dirt diamond looked like an open palm against the green carpet; above the outfield, atop the wall, he saw a guard watching the players, squatting on his heels, his rifle across his lap.

He followed the messenger past a wire-enclosed brick powerhouse that hummed and bristled and clacked with activity, and whose twin smokestacks, piercing the sky like devil's horns, dominated the entire prison. After nodding curtly to a group of men lounging on

a coal pile that flanked the powerhouse, he heard someone call: "What's up, Big Joe?" He ignored the question
and glanced at the slick-haired messenger who walked
imperiously ahead, his heels clicking against the sidewalk. He quickened his pace. The same question rose
in his throat, but he quickly swallowed it, and slowed
down his steps. He was Big Joe Noonan; he didn't
question finks who worked for the deputy. He raised
his cap, ran his hand over his kinky black hair, now
speckled with gray, then settled the cap back on his
head and lifted his chin. He was a lifer; he would wait
and see.

The buzzer sounded outside the deputy's office, and
he rose from the bench and walked over to the guard
stationed at the deputy's door. Turning his back and
raising his arms, he stood silently as the guard's hands
moved swiftly over him: under his arms, down the
center of his back, over his buttocks, between his legs,
and down to his socks. Then the guard tapped him
lightly on the shoulder and he turned and walked into
the deputy's office.

His face remained unchanged when he saw the prison
chaplain sitting behind the deputy's desk. So, this is
the pitch, he thought. Why haven't you been to church
lately, Joe? . . . well, listen to his speech, smile nice,
then go back to work. . . He moved to the front of
the desk and looked down into the bright eyes of the
chaplain. I'm here, Reverend Dickerson. . . no sweat. . .
I'll listen, no trouble. . . just rattle it off and let me get
back to work. . . Aloud he said, "You sent for me, sir?"

"Yes, Joe." The chaplain waved to a straight-backed
chair. "Sit down. I won't beat around the bush, Joe.
I'm afraid that I have some bad news for you. The
warden received a telegram today that your uncle has
died. As you know, it's my job to have to inform you
men of such things. And I'm truly sorry, Joe. I see

from your record here that your uncle is listed as your only living relative? . . ."

His eyes dropped from the chaplain's face to the shiny desk top. Dead. . . the old man dead. . . my only living relative? Ha! dead as a fish. . . look out the window. . . my only relative. . . what about my daughter they gave her away she's twenty-two now I wouldn't know her if I saw her, she wouldn't see me anyway, I killed her mother and I killedhermotherandIkilledhermother-and. . . no sweat look out the window no trouble. . . Uncle Jake dead. . . no sweat no trouble. . . listen and go back to work. . . He unfolded his arms and slowly rubbed his hands up and down his trouser legs. Then he folded his arms again across his chest.

"As you also know, Joe, it is our policy to allow a man to attend the funeral of a member of his immediate family, that is, if he can afford the expenses for himself and an accompanying guard. . ."

Uncle Jake. Dead. . . I wonder if they shaved off his gray mustache. . . I wonder if he wet the bed. . . I wonder if he was scared like I was scared of the Chair and the smell of Lysol and I killed her mother and they are dead Uncle Jake and Marta are dead. . .

". . . But, unfortunately, since your uncle resided outside the state, the usual policy does not apply. However, you will be permitted to send a message of sympathy, and flowers if you like. . ."

I should say something I should do something I should. . . flowers I should send the dead. . . and Marta liked flowers red ones and yellow ones and redandwhite and yellow. . . no sweat. . . no trouble. . . He kept his eyes on the shiny desk top and his arms folded across his chest.

"I know this is hard news, Joe," the chaplain was saying. "Perhaps you'd like to sit and talk for awhile about your uncle."

He shoved his chair back and rose. "No, thank you,

sir," he said. "But I appreciate you telling me about my uncle."

"I'm sorry, Joe."

"Thank you, sir," Joe said, turning to go.

"Oh yes, Joe, one more thing. If you want to, you can go from here directly to your cell. Perhaps you'd like to be by yourself for awhile."

"If it's all the same, sir, I'd rather go back to work."

He watched the chaplain flush and heard him say: "Suit yourself, suit yourself." Then he walked out of the deputy's office and once more followed the slick-haired messenger down the spotless sidewalk.

Uncle Jake dead and Marta dead and this slick-haired fink prancing in front of me like a woman and Marta was a woman soft and warm. . . and my daughter is a woman now. . . and Marta mourn for Uncle Jake and Reverend Dickerson mourn alone a little. . . a time to be born and a time to die and a time to mourn and a time to danceanddance and Marta danced and danced with anybody and Marta died and Uncle Jake is dead. . . Uncle Jake didn't like the visiting room and didn't visit but once a year and twenty years is time and time is time. . . time to plant Uncle Jake and Marta planted flowers yellow and white and red. . . red red like her lips and I weeped for Marta and Uncle Jake is dead and Marta danced and I weeped dancing red laughing and I criedredbloodcryingred and Marta diedcryingredcrying. . . no sweat, no trouble. . . and. . .

He turned the corner by the powerhouse and quickly stepped off the sidewalk. Four guards, their white caps gleaming in the sun, were hustling a young convict down the walk, towards the deputy's office. As they passed Joe, he saw the young man's face lifted to the sky, his black skin glistened with sweat, and blood oozed from a gash above his eye, his lips were pulled tightly over his teeth as he struggled to free himself. Joe leaned his back against the fence enclosing the powerhouse, his fingers entwined in the wire mesh. He watched the five men scuffle by silently except for their hard breathing and the scraping of their shoe soles on the concrete. For a moment his eyes locked with those of the convict, then the young man was hustled around the corner and out of sight.

As Joe stepped back onto the sidewalk he became aware of the convicts who had risen from the coal pile and were now lined up along the fence, their fingers hooked through the wire. "That kid's doing hard time. . . " "Yeah, he's got a lot to learn." "I bet he'll wear out 'fore the Hole do." "Say, did you see that lump he put on ol' Fat Ass. . ." He fell into step behind the messenger and the voices faded away.

Uncle Jake is dead and the kid is dead and got a lot to learn. . . and Marta got a lot to learn. . .and I fought 'em too twenty years ago and I died in the Hole and the Hole is still there and the kid is dead and Marta is dead red like blood and flowers flowing from the kid's head and Marta's chest. . . and twenty years the damn kid will learn that he is dead like Marta and me and UncleJakedeadweepingredbloodcrying. . . slow down kid no sweat no trouble. . .

"The chaplain told me about your uncle, Joe. Are you sure you don't want me to take you to the cellhouse?" They were at the door of the Tag Shop, and the messenger leaned against the door, looking up at Joe with an unspoken question deep in his eyes. "Nobody's in the cellhouse now; it's quiet there, and everything. . ."

"No, kid, thanks anyway."

The slick-haired messenger threw up his hand and moved off. "Maybe sometimes, Joe. See ya."

Joe stepped inside the dim Tag Shop, into the rhythmic, pulsating intensity of a hundred machines. After checking in with the shop guard, he went to his locker and hung up his cap; then he went to his stamping press and flipped on the switch. Settling himself on his stool, he picked up a stack of license plates and began to feed them, one by one, into the hungry machine. Into the right side, out the left. No sweat, no trouble.